MW01028054

YOUR WORLD-CLASS ASSISTANT

Also by Michael Hyatt

The Vision–Driven Leader:
10 Questions to Focus Your Efforts, Energize
Your Team, and Scale Your Business
(Coming 2020)

No Fail Meetings: 5 Steps to Orchestrate
Productive Meetings (and Avoid All the Rest)
(2019)

Free to Focus: A Total Productivity System
to Achieve More by Doing Less
(2019)

Your Best Year Ever: A 5–Step Plan for Achieving
Your Most Important Goals
(2018)

Living Forward: A Proven Plan to Stop Drifting
and Get the Life You Want
(with Daniel Harkavy, 2016)

Platform: Get Noticed in a Noisy World
(2012)

To Suzie and Our
World-Class Assistants

Aleshia

Becca

Elizabeth

Jamie

Jim

Renee

Shana

Susan

YOUR WORLD-CLASS ASSISTANT

Hiring, Training, and Leveraging an Executive Assistant

MICHAEL HYATT

Michael Hyatt & Company
Franklin, Tennessee

Your World-Class Assistant
Copyright © 2019 by Michael Hyatt
Published by Michael Hyatt & Company

Bulk orders for your team? Email sales@michaelhyatt.com.

ISBN: 978-1-7339701-2-9
Printed in the United States of America

MichaelHyatt.com

CONTENTS

Foreword

SUZIE BARBOUR

Senior Director of Operations, Michael Hyatt & Company

On Inauguration Day in 2017, while the rest of the world was watching the peaceful exchange of power between U.S. Presidents Obama and Trump, do you know who I was watching? The support team, those who stand beside their leaders and often go unnoticed. Why would I do that? Because I know what that support team makes possible for their leaders. I'm convinced executive assistants make the world go round. Right next to every great leader, there's usually a great EA. They manage the hundred details that allow executives to shine in key moments like that one.

I've spent most of my career leading teams of assistants: hiring them, training them, mentoring them, and watching them work their magic. Over and over, I've witnessed EAs become the heartbeat of their organizations, making their leaders' most significant contributions possible. It's been rewarding work to say the least, but if it weren't for Michael Hyatt, I wouldn't be doing it today.

Early in my career, I led a team of assistants for a company that produced arena-sized motivational events. The first time we supported an event, I met Apolo Ohno, Laura Bush, Dwyane Wade, Rudy Giuliani, Steve Forbes, and General Colin Powell. It was the coolest job, allowing our team to travel widely, work closely with prominent leaders, and tackle projects of immense scope. I learned a lot. But it cost me. The hustle required to succeed was brutal.

After years of advancing in the company and building influence in my field, everything changed. My first pregnancy ended in a devastating full-term loss. As I recovered, I tried to remember my last days carrying my son. I realized those memories were hazy because I had given all of myself to work. The week before I lost the baby, I'd put in seventy hours at work rather than savoring those moments of motherhood. I'd allowed the pace to push my personal life to the margins, and I knew it was time for a change.

I resigned soon after, but faced the same hustle culture in each subsequent role. So during my next pregnancy, I made the difficult decision to leave the career I loved to be a present parent. Perhaps you've faced that too, the choice between the work you love and the people you love.

Once my daughter was born, I loved caring for her—but still missed my work. I didn't think going back to what I'd done before was possible, so I searched for something part-time and found a virtual assistant company called Belay Solutions. They paired me with Michael Hyatt, and I began checking his email five hours per week from home. Michael was the first leader I'd ever supported who made me believe work-life balance wasn't an unattainable myth. He had faced corporate burnout himself and was building a new company with the mission to help people win at work *and* succeed at life. Not one or the other, but both. He called it the Double Win, and I was all in.

Five hours quickly grew to ten, then twenty, then thirty. Before I knew it, I was working full-time, still winning at home, and leading the most talented cadre of assistants I'd ever known.

I'll never forget the day Michael told me about his Ideal Week tool. I had spent years training EAs to be calendar management ninjas, stressing that the calendar is where the rubber meets the road and encouraging them to advocate for margin in their leaders' lives.

Michael's Ideal Week took that to a whole new level. It provided a practical framework that put all that advocacy on autopilot! It was the first time my EA philosophies would sync with Michael's productivity creations, but it wouldn't be the last. It's happened again and again over the years. Each time, that synchronicity produced new systems that changed the game for our leaders and EAs.

In the years since, our business has rapidly scaled. Once an army of one, Michael Hyatt & Company is now one of the Inc. 5000's fastest-growing private companies in America. We've achieved a lot. Yet more importantly, the dream is becoming reality for our team and clients on a daily basis. Michael would be the first to tell you that none of it would be possible without our incredible EAs.

In *Your World-Class Assistant*, Michael pulls back the curtain, giving you an inside look at how we find, hire, train, and leverage our world-class assistants to achieve great things. In the pages of this book, you'll hear not only from Michael but also from the beating heart of our business—our EA team. This is the tool I wish I'd had when my career began. And it's the book I believe will change the game for you too.

Whether you are an EA (hi friends!), have an EA, or want to hire an EA, the practical systems you're about to receive will add immense value to your career. And unlike most EA resources on the market today, Michael's approach will challenge the hustle fallacy that's been pushing you toward burnout. There is a better way.

Executive assistants make the world go round. That's especially true when they're empowered to help you win at work *and* succeed at life. So turn the page (literally and figuratively), and see what's possible!

PART 1

The Role

CHAPTER 1

Your Most Essential Hire

Imagine a tennis-ball machine stuck in overdrive. You're standing on the other side of the net, trying to return the balls as fast as they come. You're good, but, before long, balls start slipping past you. And it doesn't matter how many you hit—the number you miss keeps growing. You can't keep up.

Welcome to modern business *without* an executive assistant (EA). There are certain necessities business leaders and entrepreneurs can't afford to do without. An EA is one. I learned that the hard way.

When I was CEO of Thomas Nelson Publishers, I always had at least one EA, sometimes two, to manage logistics and other key details for me. When I left the company to pursue full-time writing, consulting, and speaking, I decided to go lean and mean. So I flew solo.

There was probably some scarcity thinking behind my decision. I had led Thomas Nelson through the Great Recession and several rounds of painful layoffs. When I left, the economy was recovering, but slowly. I was sensitive to extra overhead. What's more, I was working from my home office and had no idea where I would put an assistant. So I made the call to do without one.

It was a disaster. There were more details to manage than I'd imagined. I excelled at writing, consulting, and speaking. I was good at managing the books and enjoyed website development. But I was terrible at managing travel, expenses, and my increasingly complex calendar.

At first I tried powering through. But the tennis machine kept firing more and more balls my way. My email volume doubled within the first ninety days of entrepreneurship. More and more important messages slipped by me. Next, I tried to enlist my wife to help. Bad move. Gail was busier than I was!

Finally, I made the decision that I needed professional help. But I had some hurdles to overcome before I could implement it. I bet you can relate.

Logistics, Money, and Experience

First was logistics. As I mentioned, I had no space for an EA. I officed from home, which worked great for me. But adding another body would've required all kinds of changes. What about a virtual EA, someone working remotely? Between granting access to my calendar, email, and a dozen other services, I didn't see how that would work.

Then there was money and workload. I launched with plenty of business lined up, but money wasn't pouring in at the outset. I could almost justify the expense, but the volume of work didn't warrant hiring someone full-time. How could I get the assistance I needed at a price that made sense?

My previous experience was another hurdle. Like many leaders, I'd both good and bad experiences working with EAs over the course of my career. Sometimes that was because I'd hired the wrong assistant. Other times, it was because I didn't know how to work with an EA effectively. For example, when I was at Thomas Nelson, I had a great in-house assistant, but I realized I needed more help. I made the mistake of hiring the lowest-cost virtual assistant I could find. It was a disaster. In that case, I simply hired the wrong person. However, there had been other times when I had great assistants but still felt frustrated, mostly because I had failed to empower them. After all, there weren't any "Get the Most Out of Your EA" classes I could take.

So how did I overcome these hurdles? Well, my needs eventually overrode my reluctance. There were too many tennis balls flying at me. I desperately needed someone with another racket who could return the serve.

That led me to identify three things that I wanted to focus more of my time on: writing, consulting, and speaking. That's what drove results in my business. The more time I spent on those three activities, the more money I made.

I also identified my three biggest productivity sink-holes: booking my own travel, responding to email, and meeting with acquaintances who wanted my advice. I hated the first, felt some accomplishment with the second, and really enjoyed the third. But all three were distracting me from writing, consulting, and speaking. There were more demands than there was me!

Having identified my top three areas of focus and three greatest time drains, I started with a part-time virtual assistant from a company called Belay. It was one of the best decisions I've ever made. My remote EA started at just five hours a week. That quickly became ten hours, then fifteen, then twenty. She took more and more tasks off my plate, freeing me to work on the high-value tasks only I could do. My business grew as a result.

Eventually, I hired a full-time EA I'd met through Belay. As my business has grown, I've hired many more. Of the thirty-five current Michael Hyatt & Company employees, eight are assistants. That's 23 percent! You'll hear from them in the pages ahead and see what they make possible in my business. Before we get there, however, you need to understand the key value world-class assistants bring to our teams.

Time, Focus, and Freedom

Executive assistants empower us to leverage our two most valuable resources: time and focus. Take a look at the diagram called the Freedom Compass. It's helped point the way for tens of thousands of entrepreneurs, executives, and high-achievers just like you.

I share it in my book *Free to Focus* and in our live event and masterclass, *The Focused Leader*. It's also a core framework in our high-end coaching program, BusinessAccelerator.

Leaders regularly ask me how they can advance their most important priorities while simultaneously keeping their normal business going. I respond by

The Freedom Compass

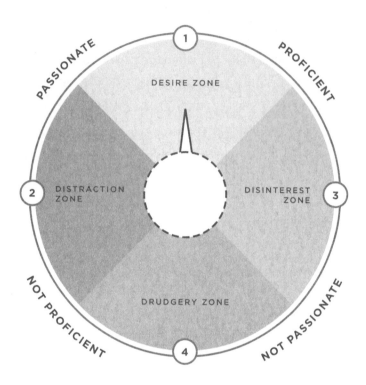

asking them to list all of their tasks, and then ask two questions of each. Ask yourself these as well:

- Am I proficient at this task?

- Am I passionate about it?

If you are proficient at a task and passionate about it, the task lands in Zone 1, what I call your Desire Zone. For me this would be writing, consulting, and speaking. Whatever it is for you, this is work you should probably be doing and not handing off to others. It's where you can make your greatest contribution, add the most benefit to yourself and to others, and feel great satisfaction in the process.

If you do something poorly and hate it, it falls into Zone 4, your Drudgery Zone. For me, this is booking travel, dealing with email, and managing my calendar. Your list may differ. But whatever these tasks are for you, they're work that slows you down. You may be able to do it, but it will take you several times longer than it would take someone else. When this work is off your plate, you feel immediate relief. Given that, you should do all you can to avoid it. It's robbing your enterprise of your best and giving it your worst.

Then there are tasks you're passionate about but not proficient at, or proficient at but not passionate about. These are Zones 2 and 3, your Distraction and Disinterest Zones. For me, these are website development and bookkeeping, respectively. If you're passionate about a task but not yet proficient, it might be excellent hobby material, but it certainly doesn't belong in your Desire Zone. If you are proficient but not passionate, you should probably hand off that work as well, though it's not as urgent as it is for Drudgery Zone activities.

The more time you spend doing things in your Desire Zone, the happier and more effective you will be. Fortunately, one person's drudgery is often another person's desire. I bet you are passionate about things that don't interest me, and proficient at things that defeat me—and vice versa. We are all wired a little differently, and that manifests in diverse backgrounds, interests, and skills.

How does that relate to the EA question? I don't enjoy or excel at repetitive tasks or maintaining systems. They tax my attention and wear me down. I find them draining. But some people find them energizing. Others find them soothing.

We bring different things to, and get different things from, our work. That goes for both leaders and their EAs. There's endless variety in the people who want to serve as assistants. But those who seek it out tend to do so because the mix of tasks particular to EA work appeals to them. They are both passionate about and proficient in them. It's their Desire Zone!

Whether you're thinking of getting an EA or currently underutilizing your assistant, I'm confident *Your World-Class Assistant* will show you how an EA can free you to focus on your Desire Zone, keep you out of your Drudgery Zone, and help you maintain the focus that drives results in your business.

It is important to say that your Freedom Compass represents an ideal. Almost no one works exclusively in their Desire Zone. But it is possible. Today I rarely work outside my Desire Zone, and EAs are one reason why.

Who Needs an EA?

Not everyone needs an EA, but many more of us could benefit from their assistance than you might think. If you list all of your tasks at work and the vast majority of them fall into Desire Zone activities, maybe you can do without the help. But if you're regularly working in your Drudgery Zone, you definitely need to get help with the tasks holding you back.

When it comes down to it, there are four key indicators you either need an EA or need to better utilize the one you have.

Indicator 1: You're Overwhelmed

It can be really hard, when you are in the thick of it, to step back and evaluate. So if you're up to your eyeballs in work, I've got a hard-won secret for you: There are only twenty-four hours in a day. Nothing you do will add one more second. But how you spend those hours will determine the quality of the work and ideas you bring to the table. We all have seasons when there's more work than time, seasons when we have to push through and make it happen. But they should be seasons—as in, periods that eventually stop.

If being regularly overwhelmed is the norm for you, if you're trying to do everything on your own, you will drown in your own success. To be at the top of your game, you need to be alert, healthy, and clear headed. You can't do that if you're constantly worried about returning all the balls coming your direction.

Being overwhelmed doesn't make you a bad person. It's a sign of your success. An EA carrying some of the burden can help ensure that success continues.

Indicator 2: You're Distracted by Administrative Stuff

When you go it alone, you have to do everything. If you need to book an airline ticket, you go online to do it. If you need to make an appointment, you pick up the phone or send an email. But if you want to maximize time in your Desire Zone, this one-person routine is not sustainable.

You may think, "Well, I've done this before. I can do it competently. I'll just power through." But consider two things. First, just because you can do something doesn't mean it's the best use of your time. If my compensation is, say, fifty dollars an hour and I'm still doing tasks that someone making fifteen dollars an hour can do just as well or better, it's a better use of company resources to have that person do it instead.

Second, not every leader needs to be an administrative genius. Many of us simply are not wired that way. It's time we embrace our unique style of leadership and stop feeling shame around the tasks we find draining. Even if you're a leader who excels at administrative work—and some do—you've probably discovered that taking on too much of it pulls you away from the visionary contribution you need to make. It's not the best use of your time. Whether administrative tasks fall into your Drudgery Zone or your Distraction Zone, it's time to up your game with an EA.

◀ *EA Mistake No. 1* ▶

Undervaluing Our True Worth

How valuable is your time? Most of us don't know, which is why we keep wasting so much of it on activities that don't really matter. Without a doubt, this is the number-one mistake people make with their EAs. Take your total compensation and divide it across your available work hours. Now ask yourself: Is mailing that package, scheduling that meeting, or processing those invoices really worth that amount of time? I bet not, especially when you count the opportunity cost. If we really understood how much we're worth, we'd hand off far more work to our EAs.

Indicator 3: You're Not Focusing on Your Strengths

There are certain things that only you can do. No one can give a presentation like you do. No one can negotiate contracts, make the pitch, or create new products like you do.

Whatever type of business you are in, there are some things that only you can accomplish. If you're not focused on these, you're in trouble. If you've never had an assistant, you might think the goal is to clone yourself. That's a mistake. The point is not for you to do less of *everything*. The point is to do less of what others can do for you.

I identified writing, speaking, and consulting as the three ways I added unique value to my company. I knew I could delegate the rest. Why are you spending your valuable time doing things an EA could help you accomplish? A good rule of thumb is that if you can teach someone else to do a task, you shouldn't spend your time doing it. Your EA should be doing it.

Indicator 4: You Feel Too Stressed to Get Help

Productivity isn't just about doing more stuff. It's about doing the right stuff. Trying to squeeze more tasks into an already cramped day is a productivity killer, especially if they're the wrong kind of tasks. When you ask the two Freedom Compass questions about your current task list, I bet you'll find many of them are.

If you're honest with yourself, you could probably list three to five things *right now* that are hindering you from maximizing the time you have. You don't need more to do. You need better-ordered time to invest in the things that will help you achieve your personal and organizational objectives.

Stress is caused by a lot of things. One of them is feeling like you can't get ahead no matter how hard you work. But that's not the case, and there is a simple solution: stop. Stop telling yourself that. Stop trying to do everything. Stop burdening yourself with your own false sense of inadequacy. Let somebody else work on the things that are slowing you down.

The Magic of Margin

When you hire an EA, you're not just adding people hours. You're redeeming time for yourself and adding more margin to your life. You can't spend every day working at full burn, even if the work is in your Desire Zone. You'll flame out. And it won't take all that long. The very thing you love to do will become the thing you hate doing most.

Margin is like a savings account, but instead of money, it's full of creativity, energy, psychological well-being, and perspective. Without margin, you will not bring the best ideas to the table. You will not continue to innovate. You will not be able to anticipate what's coming, or even recognize when things aren't going well. And, on top of it all, you'll either lose your business or get fried.

Margin doesn't just happen. You have to fight for it. Everyone, it seems, wants a piece of you. And no one seems to appreciate the fact that you are a finite resource. Perhaps you don't even realize it. Yet you are finite, and if you don't keep some of yourself in reserve, you'll come up empty when you need new ideas or extra energy. You'll be maxed out.

If you find yourself maxed out with work, you're probably not able to bring much to the table in your personal life either. I've certainly faced seasons where work was requiring so much that I neglected my health and most important relationships. Finding some margin by delegating some of your tasks to an EA will free you up to produce greater results in your business—and those results will likely overflow into your personal life as well.

It's worth asking yourself a few questions at this point:

- What is my lack of focus and the accompanying loss of productivity costing my business?

- What could I be doing with the time if I weren't buried in administrative detail?

- What could I create that would truly advance my business if I didn't feel so overwhelmed?

- Could an EA, even a part-time EA, help me create the margin I need to get ahead and get my life back?

Based on the needs these questions usually surface, I've found that it's not just executives or CEOs who need EAs. Authors, coaches, consultants, creatives, doctors, entrepreneurs, nonprofit leaders, school administrators, government leaders, lawyers, pastors, and speakers—there's a long list of people in all kinds of professions who could benefit from executive assistance.

EAs have turned my company into a well-oiled machine. They keep the leadership team focused on what we do best, ensuring we make our greatest contribution to the business. In fact, almost every leader on my team has an EA who manages their email inbox, controls their calendar, and submits their expense reports. And that's just the beginning. Our EAs do much more!

In a pinch, they'll pick up our dry cleaning, but they'll also do business tasks that you might not think of as EA work. These are things like managing meetings, advanced itinerary planning, and project management. They also keep our company from becoming too bureaucratic. You don't need quite as many processes when you have a small team of EAs who keep things moving. And when a process is needed, it can be structured organically. The EAs bring the need to our attention and usually help us think through how to implement it. Often they build and implement the processes themselves.

Despite the vast number of people who could benefit from having an executive assistant, I've noticed that many are reluctant to take the plunge. Just as bad, I've talked with many people who have an EA but don't know how to make the most of the position. As a result, they miss getting the help they need. Maybe that's you. If so, I've got good news. In the chapters that follow, I'll show you how to hire, train, and leverage an EA for maximum results.

Chapter 2 will walk you through the basic tasks any EA can handle for you. You'll learn the ins and outs of delegating email, phone calls, vendor communications and more. More important, we'll bust the twin myths that you can't *afford* an EA and don't *need* one. You'll finally get over the limiting belief that you can't trust another person to do a share of your work.

Chapter 3 will open your mind to the greater possibilities that a great EA can create for you. You'll see how handing over your calendar, meeting agendas, and travel plans can eliminate the chaos and restore the margins of your time. We'll also talk about project management, content creation, candidate screening, and a host of other tasks that the right EA can handle as well or better than you can. You'll begin to get excited about the prospect of finding your first EA, or delegating a lot more work to your current one.

Chapter 4 will equip you to find and hire the right assistant. We'll begin by showing you how to make the case—even to yourself—that hiring an EA makes good financial sense. And you'll gain great tips for finding the right person and insight on the question of hiring an in-person versus a remote assistant. Finally, you'll learn the four must-have characteristics you need in any EA. When we're done, you'll feel competent to begin the search for your own world-class assistant.

Chapter 5 will give you the basics for starting a new EA relationship. You'll learn how to determine which tasks to delegate and how to communicate your expectations and preferences. You'll gain invaluable tools for collecting and communicating key information, and get an itinerary for your first ninety days. This chapter will give you the confidence to pull the trigger on hiring, knowing that you're set up for success.

Chapter 6 will equip you with a standard rhythm for communicating with your EA. You'll learn what to communicate, when, how, and how often. As a result, you both will always have the most up-to-date information, manage expectations well, and avoid the frustrations that can sour an EA relationship. This chapter also teaches you the basics of delegation, including the stages of delegation, the five levels of delegation, and the pitfalls of abdicating your authority as a leader. With this solid framework, you'll be ready to take your EA relationship to the next level.

Chapter 7 will bring all these threads together, giving you a vision for what you can accomplish with an EA. The result? Freedom.

Finally, I've included a link to some downloadable resources to make your EA experience more productive: sample templates and frameworks discussed in these chapters, along with a list of apps and services. Together, you will accomplish more than you ever thought possible.

You can't hit all the tennis balls back over the net, nor do you need to. If you hire an EA or begin fully utilizing the one you have, you'll return the shots only you can make and improve your game along the way. With a world-class EA, you'll have the best chance of winning day in and out, week after week, year after year.

CHAPTER 2

What an Executive Assistant Can Do for You

The Basics

When I coach leaders on hiring an executive assistant, they sometimes tell me, "I don't need a secretary," or, "I can't afford a secretary." *Need* and *afford* are both relative terms, but the really tricky word in those sentences is *secretary*.

People often forgo an EA or underutilize the one they have because they confuse the role with that of a secretary. That term can sometimes represent an outdated vision that limits the scope and possibility of an

EA's contribution to repetitive clerical work. It sounds like something out of a black-and-white movie, where every executive wears a suit and has a stenographer sitting in the outer office. EAs regularly handle clerical work, of course. But as you'll see here and in the next chapter, an EA can do much more for you and your business. In fact, given what a properly trained and equipped EA makes possible, you might be forced to rethink your definitions of *need* and *afford*.

These two chapters are about the scope of EA work, looking at the problems they can solve for busy achievers. In this chapter, I'll cover the basics. In the next, we'll look at more advanced techniques.

Most of the basic and advanced techniques work with both full-time and part-time EAs, in either remote or in-person positions—though there are limits. If you hire a virtual EA at ten hours a week (which is a great place to start), they won't be able to match what someone working alongside you for forty hours a week can accomplish.

Managing Communications

The first task an EA should tackle is managing communications, particularly email. But that could also include phone, social media, and more. Your EA represents you by communicating your messages to others.

Handling Email

There is nothing worse than walking out of a meeting, looking down at your phone, and seeing emails numbering in double digits awaiting your response. If you travel much, the number can be even higher. It takes hours to process all of those messages, and you probably have no extra time to do it.

Good news: Your EA can monitor your email accounts and even handle responses on your behalf. If you effectively communicate your expectations, you'll be surprised at how much email gets processed while you're focused on your Desire Zone. When handing this off to an EA, it helps if you already have a system in place. If you don't, I encourage you to get one—and an EA can help you with that too.

In my company, we mostly use Spark for email. (See the Resources section at the back for a description of this and the other apps and services we use.) Spark allows my EA, Jim Kelly, to answer on my behalf using a bank of email templates we've created. He can also assign messages to me or other people on my team so we can post messages to one another privately within Spark before forming a response to the sender.

When I talk with executives and entrepreneurs about letting someone else manage their email, they're often reluctant. They feel like they're losing control of something important. I felt that way at first too, but is email really all that important? Ask yourself the questions from Chapter 1.

- Am I proficient at this task?

- Am I passionate about it?

Another way to phrase the questions might be this: Is this the most profitable and enjoyable use of my time? Or: Could I produce better results for my business if I focused on something else?

If email is in your Desire Zone, carry on. But for most leaders I know, email is in one of the other zones. Most just find it annoying or overwhelming; it's in their Drudgery Zone. Others are really good at it, but they find it draining or boring; it's in their Disinterest Zone. Still others use their email to escape harder, more valuable work; it's in their Distraction Zone.

If that sounds like you, it's time to hand your inbox over to your assistant. Even if all they do is screen out the trivia and flag the important stuff for you, you'll see some benefit. Eliminating time spent on emails that don't need your personal attention frees more time to respond to the ones that move your business forward.

Multiple Inboxes. One tactic I recommend is using several inboxes. If you can, you really want three. A personal email account, a private work account, and a public work account. Ideally, your EA operates your public work account and very few people know about the others.

◄ *EA Power Tip No. 1* ►

Give Your EA Access to Your Email

RENEE MURPHY
Executive Assistant to Jarrod Souza, CFO

Many leaders are drowning in email. They'd love to get it off their plate but think handing it off is too daunting a task—or that an EA could never handle it the way they'd want it done. But you can delegate email to your EA in phases and still win back tons of time.

Start by just sharing email with them—as in, let them "shadow" your inbox activity so they can see what's coming in and how you respond. When Jarrod and I began our EA relationship, having visibility into his email helped orient me to his world and priorities. After learning how he handled the inbox, it wasn't long before I could filter the important email from the rest. That saved him a lot of time.

Once I'd been working with him for a while, I was able to begin answering some—then most—emails for him, saving him even more time and energy. By working in phases, you can start saving time now and build up your assistant's ability to manage your inbox with excellence.

Email Templates. In addition to multiple inboxes, using templates will help you effectively delegate email to your assistant. If you already have a set of templates you use, share those with your EA. If not, no problem. Make a list of the templates you want and have your assistant create first drafts. Then all you have to do is edit them. Regardless of your industry, there are some common requests that most leaders receive. It's helpful to have a standard response to each of these in your vault. Here are some examples of requests I get often.

First, "Can I pick your brain?" This also sounds like, "Can we meet for coffee?" In my experience, the frequency of this request is directly proportional to your success. The more you win, the more people want informal access to your insight. While I always want to help people, most of these requests come from distant acquaintances. Most also lack clarity around the outcome they want. It all adds up to an unproductive use of my time and theirs. So I've empowered my EA with a polite decline that redirects the individual to some of my free resources, like my website or podcast, and, if they're really serious, conveys my rates for paid consulting. Whatever approach you take, arm your assistant with an answer to brain-picking requests.

Second, "Can you come to this event?" High achievers and heavy calendars go hand-in-hand. When the requests are flooding in, you'll save a ton of time by simply telling your assistant which ones to accept and which to decline—without rehashing the wording for each. The real sweet spot here is when your assistant knows how to answer many of those requests without even asking you. More to come on that later, but, for now, arm them with template answers to accept and decline invitations.

Third, "Can you tell me your (mailing address, phone number, office hours, etc.)?" This one seems simple, but typing out your mailing address every time someone wants to send you a package adds up to a lot of wasted time by year's end. Make sure your EA has templates to answer this request for basic contact information. Check the Resources section at the end of this book to download (and swipe) our email templates. They're yours for the taking.

You can store your templates as documents, drafts, or even email signatures. (Yes, you can have twenty different signatures, each containing a full template reply that you select from a drop-down list!) Some email management programs also have a built-in function to insert "canned responses" with a single click. My team has utilized programs like Spark, Gmail, and Groove over the years with great success. Whichever format you choose, the benefit remains the same. Your assistant can rapidly reply to common requests. Plus, you can rest assured that they're answering those requests the way you'd answer them. Templates offer instant quality control, no micromanagement required.

Handling Calls and Voicemail

The multiple inbox trick also works well for phones. If you're in an office with a phone system, have your EA pick up for you. But don't stop there. Have you ever found yourself slogging through voicemail, fully aware that you don't have time to return even half the calls? It's paralyzing. Instead, have your EA gather the voice messages, review them with you in one phone call or meeting, and then relay your response to each party. What might have cost an hour or more of your time can be reduced to five or ten minutes.

What if you're not in an office with a traditional phone system? The answer for most entrepreneurs is similar to email. You need one line for personal and private work use and another for public use. The trick is to give that second number to your EA and never answer it yourself.

One way to do this is with a Google Voice number. Keep your private number for family, friends, and key colleagues. Give the Google number to everyone else. If you download the Google Voice app for your phone, you can set it to forward texts and voicemail to your email inbox—where your EA can easily field those messages.

As for other platforms and channels of communication, think through how you might include your EA. Can they handle your social media inboxes? Can they keep track of conversations in Slack, Asana, and so on? If the answer isn't an obvious yes, then ask what would have to be true to get to yes. Even if you don't know the answer, your assistant likely does.

The less time you spend in tasks where your passion and proficiency run low, the better. There are only 168 hours in a week. How much do you really want to spend on email or voicemail when you have more substantial goals to pursue? By delegating communications to someone who possesses real passion and proficiency, you're free to work in your Desire Zone—and so are they. And it's important to note, that same principle holds for other potential EA tasks.

Vendors, Expenses, and Information Management

These days, it makes more and more sense to work with outside vendors for a range of services that once were commonly done in-house. There are many benefits to this shift but also some challenges.

One is the growing number of contracts, invoices, and the like. If your EA is handling communication with a vendor, why not all the paperwork? Again, ask yourself: Do I have proficiency and passion for this task? Is it the most profitable and enjoyable use of my time?

A good EA will do this better than you can. They can gather the invoices for you to review and approve, and then make sure whoever handles your accounting is aware the invoices are ready to be paid. Paying people on time—including your suppliers—builds trust and respect. Falling behind, or just being inconsistent, creates a reputation you want to avoid.

You likely have your own invoices to issue as well. Unless you send these on a timely basis—and follow up—you won't get paid. And nothing can ruin your day faster than discovering you are in a cash-flow crunch simply because you forgot to bill clients on time. An EA can handle all these details, from issuing the original invoice to tracking payments to making collection calls. This can generate even more revenue, because you are now free to focus on finding more clients and generating more business.

What about expense reports? There is nothing like coming back from a week of travel and having to wade through a stack of receipts and notes. It's necessary. You need it so your accountant can create reimbursement requests and file the necessary documentation for tax purposes. But it can take an entire day if you travel a lot or regularly make purchases around town for business. It's the same as any other task evaluation: Are expense reports one of the things that only you can do for your business? I didn't think so. You're better off letting your EA sort through the details so you can focus on higher leverage opportunities.

Finally, there's the broader question of information management. Entering new database records, tagging records, or organizing drives, folders, and lists can be time consuming and even intellectually taxing work. And some of us are better at it than others. Thankfully, your EA can help with your information management needs, including CRMs, digital archives, survey collection, and so on. In Chapter 6, we'll cover delegation processes and tools to make this simple and straightforward.

Errands, Gifts, and More

You can buy everything from rabbits to routers online. There's no reason your EA can't order office supplies, computers, printers, gifts for your loved ones or clients, research materials, samples, or even submit online work orders for printing and binding for your next presentation. If they're local, they can pick up items like this from a store. If they're virtual, they can have them shipped or arrange for a local courier. If you empower them with your account information and some of your preferences, they have all they need to process all sorts of tasks like this on your behalf, often with little to no involvement from you.

In time, your EA will begin to anticipate your needs. One of our EAs, Aleshia Curry is so good at this that it's become a running joke. When people send her a request, there's a good chance she's already taken care of it. Aleshia's famous for writing back with the hashtag, "#alreadydone." I'll give you some helpful tools for getting your EA the relevant data they need to make these kinds of calls in Chapter 5.

Avoid Berlin Walls

While you're in rethinking mode for using EAs, here's something else to keep in mind: the

Berlin Wall. That's my name for the mistaken idea that EAs should see to only their boss's professional needs and not to any nonprofessional concerns.

Don't misunderstand this point. If the company is paying for it, the bulk of an EA's work should be related to the company, and there are things you shouldn't expect of EAs. They aren't hired for their cooking, cleaning, or childcare services, to pick a few obvious don'ts.

However, let's say that dry cleaning really needs to be picked up, but you have to study numbers and notes to prepare for a presentation to your board or to potential investors. Is it okay to ask your EA to do that, even if most of what got dry cleaned are Hawaiian shirts for your upcoming vacation? Absolutely.

Or let's look briefly at calendars. (We'll cover this in more detail in the next chapter.) Your schedule is a holistic thing. Date night, school events for the kids, medical appointments, lunch meetings, concerts, haircuts, travel, and church events require coordination, both with themselves and with your work schedule. Otherwise, chaos. So it makes sense to have your EA coordinate personal and family events as well.

One of the ways I've leaned on an EA to help me win both at home and at work is by having them manage my weekly date nights with Gail. I used to get so busy with work during the week that I'd forget to make reservations or keep the time blocked on my calendar. If I did remember, it often pulled me away from key projects during the work day. Instead, I've shared with Jim, my EA, that date nights are a huge priority for me. He's helped me protect them. He handles the reservations, buys flowers, and makes sure everything important is noted in the calendar event, including a standard set of date night questions for us to discuss:

- Share one win from this week in the following areas: work, marriage, and parenting.

- What's the biggest challenge you faced this week?

- What's one thing I could do to serve you or honor you in the coming week?

- If we do nothing else right as a family this week, what's the one thing we should be sure to focus on?

- What's something you're afraid of right now?

- What's something you're really excited about right now?

- What's something you've been dreaming about lately?

- Share something special that you notice about each other this week.

Jim's help in this area has automated one of my most important priorities, ensuring that it happens regularly and taking the pressure off of Gail and me when it comes to scheduling and decision making. This, in turn, keeps me from being distracted by last-minute date night prep when I'm tackling a critical project at work.

The Berlin Wall—a rigid division between professional and private life—is counterproductive to advancing you and your company's most important objectives. It is not in the interest of the company for you to pick up your own dry cleaning if it means that you perform worse at a key meeting. By taking that off your plate, your EA is actually adding to the bottom line. And because a schedule should cover more than your working hours, tearing down that wall will make you less likely to just do it all yourself when you should be letting an EA handle it for you.

In the next chapter, we'll dive deeper into the ways your EA can tame your chaotic calendar, along with several other advanced EA techniques.

CHAPTER 3

What an Executive Assistant Can Do for You

Advanced Techniques

Once I had a job without executive support, but it did offer significant performance bonuses. So I made a wager with myself. I hired an executive assistant out of my own pocket, betting that it would allow me to perform at an even higher level. I couldn't tell my employer at the time because he would have shut me down. That meant I didn't have the freedom to really optimize the position. Even so, I was convinced that even partial EA support would help me deliver bigger, better results.

The wager paid off. Confirming my hunch, I was far more productive with an EA. I earned more than enough in bonuses to cover the expense, and I proved the value of the position to my boss. Using the advanced EA techniques I reveal in this chapter, you, too, can put the odds in your favor.

Calendar Management

One of the biggest mistakes in business is managing your own calendar. It's like the old line about the lawyer who takes himself as a client. Nothing good comes of it. You will always overestimate the number of meetings and appointments you can handle, and underestimate the time needed for nearly every task. You will eat up your week with calls and meetings, and suddenly there will be insufficient time left for productive work.

Worse, as the requests start flying at you, you'll likely slip into reactive mode. You'll end up agreeing to more work than you should and fail to align your schedule with what's most important in life, including your goals, key projects, and deadlines. All of a sudden, you'll find yourself cramming that important work into nights and weekends so you can accommodate the meetings you now regret accepting in the first place.

And what happens if you wake up sick, need to

reschedule afternoon appointments due to a family emergency, or get stuck in a meeting that runs long? If you're the only one looking at your calendar, you'll also be the one responsible for making those adjustments on the fly.

You need someone who can run interference and look out for your interests, and arrange them in the right priority better than you can do for yourself. You need an agent for your time. You need an EA to manage your calendar. This important task comes down to two key activities: appointment booking and calendar proofing.

Booking Appointments

If you've ever tried to book your own appointments, you know just how time consuming it can be. Arranging a single meeting can produce a string of fifteen emails. Then you're even further behind. Even if you use a scheduling app like Calendly to make the process easier, you still have to do a good amount of work on the front end to ensure you're actually opening up the right slots for others to book time with you. An EA will keep balance in your schedule and quickly make adjustments when necessary.

For starters, an EA can ask these key questions about meeting requests:

- Is this meeting necessary?

- Do I need to be there?

- Will other required parties be there also (so we don't waste time)?

- What preparation is needed, and do I have adequate time for that?

A good EA can also evaluate the worth of standing meetings and help you decide which meetings you can safely exit. Since the EA has visibility across your entire calendar—professional and personal—they can ensure you're not double booked, needlessly booked, or shorting your margin in order to attend.

A useful tool for your EA to book appointments is the Ideal Week. I've used this tool for years now. You can learn more about it in my book *Free to Focus*, but here are the basics. Calendar management is more than traffic control. The way I see it, you make a basic life choice when you set your calendar. You can either live on purpose, according to a plan you've set. Or you can live by accident, reacting to the demands of others. The first approach is proactive; the second is reactive, and far less effective.

Granted, you can't plan for everything. Things happen that you couldn't have anticipated. But it is a whole lot easier to accomplish what matters most when you are proactive and begin with the end in mind. The

Ideal Week lets you do this. It's similar to a financial budget. The difference is that you plan how you will spend your *time* rather than your *money*.

In my Ideal Week—the week I would live if I could control 100 percent of what happens—has a theme for each day.

Monday is devoted to my team, both one-on-one meetings and leadership meetings. This includes a one-on-one meeting with my EA. (More on that in Chapter 5.) This is what I call a Back Stage day: a day during which I'm doing essential work but mostly meeting, preparing, and maintenance.

Tuesday and Wednesday are what I call Front Stage days. These are days for my highest-leverage work, the work necessary to make progress on our goals and key projects.

Thursday is an ad hoc day. I use it for whatever is most important that week. However, the one thing I don't schedule is meetings of any kind. That's because we observe a company-wide No Meetings Thursday to really focus on our work. You can find out more in my book *No Fail Meetings*.

Friday is another Back Stage day, this time reserved for external meetings.

Saturday is an Off Stage day, reserved for personal chores and activities.

Sunday is another Off Stage day, set aside for church, rest, and planning the next week.

These themed days are further segmented into blocks of time, some of which shouldn't budge without a good reason. For example, my morning ritual is very important to my day. So are my workday start-up and shut-down routines. And I have a hard deadline of 6:00 p.m. to leave work behind for the night. That's necessary to preserve the margin that is so precious to me each evening.

The whole idea of an Ideal Week is captured by the word *ideal*. It's the kind of week you would plan if you had total control of your time and could engineer a week for maximum productivity. Like any ideal, it's useful in that it helps guide and direct the imperfect. An Ideal Week serves as a target or standard by which to judge incoming requests. You won't hit it every time, but by using it as a scheduling tool, you'll come a lot closer to it than you probably are now.

I highly recommend that you map out your own Ideal Week and share it with your EA as a basic template for helping to design the rhythm of your weeks. That way, you are both working from the same set of expectations. In fact, I think this is so important that anytime we hire a new EA at my company, we've added a standard exercise as part of the interview process. We ask them to design a sample Ideal Week for the leader they'll be working with. They've all passed with flying colors!

How does the Ideal Week affect booking appointments? Here's a great example from one of the leaders in our company, John Meese. He said, "One of my personal goals this year is to adhere to my Ideal Week with eighty percent consistency. In the past, I've found that to be very difficult as needs change—and everything feels urgent all the time. But when I get it right, then I have my most effective weeks as a leader, so I know it's worth it."

He and his EA, Elizabeth White, use the Ideal Week as a pre-authorization. "If a meeting or appointment fits into my Ideal Week and existing commitments," John said, "Elizabeth is free to schedule the appointment without checking with me first. If the meeting is less than twenty-four hours away, she lets me know directly. If not, I'll discover it on my calendar or during our weekly one-on-one meeting."

What if a meeting or appointment falls outside the parameters of his Ideal Week? "She needs to get my approval first," he says. "That could be as simple as a quick text or a thumbs up from me in Slack, but that one extra step is just enough to eliminate the majority of scheduling conflicts between my real week and my Ideal week."

This methodology has enabled him to reach 80 to 90 percent compliance with his Ideal Week, which means a week designed for ideal margin and maximum productivity. What would that look like for you, and what would it mean for your business, to have that kind of success?

◄ *EA Mistake No. 2* ►

Undervaluing the EA's Worth

Some of us don't fully appreciate the competence, talents, and skills of our EAs. We don't trust them enough to delegate the important but time-consuming tasks that take us off mission. We don't take the time to ask for their input on how to improve our systems or believe them when they say they can handle something on our behalf. The truth is that an EA is really a full partner in achieving our goals. We just have to be willing to learn about their unique skill set, value it, then empower them to use it fully within our business.

Calendar Proofing

What's more annoying than driving across town to find that the person you were supposed to meet had the day wrong? "Sorry, I thought it was Tuesday, not Monday. Silly me." Now you've wasted time that could have been spent on something more productive than sipping coffee by yourself.

An EA can keep your appointments trued-up so you don't waste time chasing down schedule changes, cancellations, or no-shows. Another benefit of having someone confirm your appointments is adding a personal touch to the process. When someone takes the time to confirm an appointment via phone or email, it communicates that the commitment is important. And it is important, if for no other reason than that you're parting with thirty minutes or an hour of your valuable time.

Our team of EAs all do some form of calendar proofing for their leaders, and it's something I highly recommend. My EA, Jim, does this on Wednesdays or Thursdays because he's usually confirming meetings with external people for the following week. Sometimes he works even further out, depending on necessity.

Jim follows a calendar proofing process with a simple template. There's a link to it in the Resources section. Jim goes item by item through the calendar and confirms that times, places, and other key information (such as flight confirmation numbers) are correct. If all's well, he indicates that with a check mark. If there are errors or gaps, he notes that as well, along with what he's doing to rectify or confirm. He highlights those items so he can easily find them again.

The more complex your schedule, the more important it is to have this level of proofing. Jim admits it's a little tedious but says using the proofing template is vital. It allows him to keep a bird's-eye view of the entire schedule. That enables him to catch conflicts or omissions he might miss if working only with the calendar entries. Calendar proofing ensures I'm on time and in the know, ready for whatever's on the docket.

◄ *EA Power Tip No. 2* ►

Hold a Monthly Calendar Preview Meeting

SHANA SMITH

*Executive Assistant to Suzie Barbour,
Sr. Director of Operations*

Most leaders have crazy calendars. Whether it's a big meeting at work or a spouse's birthday, important events can sneak up and leave you feeling underprepared. Even if you're doing a calendar review in your weekly one-on-one, you probably have time only to look a week or two ahead. If you don't take time to look further out, you can become disconnected from larger deadlines. A monthly calendar preview meeting is the perfect solution. How does it work?

Your EA walks through your schedule for the coming month or quarter, week by week. Together, you ensure that nothing important is left out, that nothing has been double booked, and that you have adequate time to prepare for each commitment.

The leader can even include their spouse in that meeting to make sure their personal priorities are aligned. As a bonus, you also have this opportunity to delegate tasks to your assistant as you go—like making a reservation for a birthday dinner or providing research you'll need for a meeting. By previewing your calendar with your assistant each month, you'll be set up for success with your most important commitments!

Managing Meetings

How many times have you had a big meeting sneak up on you because the days leading up to it were fully booked with other things? When that happens, it's easy to find yourself working the weekend or staying up late the night before to prepare. Another meeting pain point is walking out of meetings with a ton of notes and action items to process but no capacity to follow up. Your EA can solve that problem for you.

Scheduling is just the beginning. Your EA can do much more to make meetings more productive. In addition to scheduling meetings, your EA can also be involved in your meetings. In fact, a good EA can do a far better job of managing a meeting than some executives I know. Your EA can create an agenda and distribute it to attendees before the meeting, gather the documents you need and book preparation time on your calendar, and even help you think through key ideas in advance.

Your EA can also facilitate the meeting, whether it's in person or virtual. That includes scheduling space for the meeting and arranging any catering or special equipment that may be needed. Our EAs often call the meeting to order, then hand the agenda over to the leader.

As the meeting progresses, the EA will take notes and assign action items in Asana, which is the task management system we use, then follow up to ensure completion. They also serve as a timekeeper to ensure that all agenda items are covered in the time allotted, sometimes calling for a halt to discussion so a decision can be made. And the meeting never ends without the EA summarizing the decisions made and action items assigned.

I talk a lot about creating a great meeting experience in my book *No Fail Meetings*, and EAs play a vital role in this.

◀ *EA Power Tip No. 3* ▶

Bring Your EA to Meetings

JAMIE HESS
Executive Assistant to Megan Hyatt Miller, COO

Meetings eat up a lot of time for most leaders. And a lot of leaders struggle to lead the meeting while keeping track of notes and action items. Bringing your EA along is the ultimate fix. They can be responsible for capturing top takeaways and sending them to you later.

They can also drive execution on the action items—whether that's scheduling a time for you to complete your tasks or following up with other people on their items. Plus, having your EA present allows you to be fully focused on participating and contributing great ideas. You can make your meetings exponentially more productive by including your EA.

Travel

Business travel can be fun and beneficial, or it can become one of the most frustrating and negative experiences of your week. Even if you travel only occasionally, you know how much time it takes to find a good flight and fare, one that will get you there and back on time without eroding your margin, busting the budget, or leaving you exhausted. Then there's ground transportation, hotel and restaurant reservations, rewards programs, and a dozen other details to arrange. If you travel often, keeping up with those details amounts to a part-time job. You need the support of an EA.

If arranging your own travel is cumbersome when you're in the office, how much more difficult is it when you're stranded by a canceled flight or weather delay? On your own, that can be a significant problem to navigate, not to mention a huge point of stress. But your EA can be the one-call solution, allowing you to relax and focus on your priorities while the changes are sorted out.

For travel at Michael Hyatt & Company, including personal travel, our EAs both book the reservations and handle other trip details, as well as creating an Event Briefing that places all that information in the executive's hands. You can find a link to our Event Briefing Template in the Resources section. It includes things like travel dates and flight times, hotel address and confirmation numbers, restaurant reservations, contact information for any meeting, and a trip itinerary including travel time to airports and appointments and time zone changes. Our assistants look up the weather forecast and offer tips on what clothing to pack.

All of that information is placed into a Google Doc, which can be accessed by phone or computer. This level of preparation removes most of the stress of being on the road. Thanks to my EA, all the information I need is always at my fingertips. And I have a one-call solution in case of any complications.

Other Tasks

The list of tasks that might fill an EAs day are as varied as your needs and their passions and proficiencies. Don't forget, the Freedom Compass works for your assistant too. It can help both of you identify the specific tasks that can be deleted from your Drudgery Zone and added to their Desire Zone. That said, here are some additional tasks that an EA might handle for you, depending on your needs and their competencies.

Research and Recommendations

Research, reporting, and fact checking burn up time. If you're not familiar with where to go or what you're looking for, it can be a huge drain on your time and energy. Fortunately, this is work that can easily be given to someone who enjoys managing details and understands your expectations. Leaders are in the business of making decisions, not necessarily doing the legwork required to get there. With the help of an EA, you can gather the information you need to make a choice without spending hours in research.

Goal Tracking and Project Management

Some leaders like to manage their own projects. But even those who are proficient at this often find that their time is better spent elsewhere. Tracking tasks, prompting action, following up on delegation: all these are things your EA can do for you. You can receive status updates during your weekly one-on-one or sprint planning. Rather than staring at a spreadsheet or project plan, you can focus on decision making and motivating the team.

In addition to serving an executive, some of our EAs also function as project managers for their entire team. When team members realize that the EA is empowered to manage a project on your behalf, they'll receive a high level of trust and cooperation.

Content Creation

Content creation is a core activity for professionals such as authors, consultants, and speakers. Yet all business leaders must create some content for things like reports, presentations, speeches, and project proposals. That's not to mention content marketing through blogs and social media.

The problem is that many business leaders are neither passionate nor proficient in crafting written documents, presentations, or other forms of content. For some, this is squarely in their Drudgery Zone. For others it may simply be a distraction or an item of disinterest.

Your EA can help you save vast amounts of time here. At the most basic level, they can transcribe oral material for written form, gather research, or generate a rough draft based on your objectives. Some EAs will have the expertise to write speeches, draft important emails, generate social media posts, or create compelling presentations.

Areas of Unique Expertise

Most EAs have passion and proficiency around administrative tasks like email, calendar management, and facilitating meetings. But remember that each EA comes with unique skills and life experiences that may go beyond your initial vision for their contribution. Even if the EA work is the only work they've done, it's likely that they've served a variety of leaders in various industries. If you need some help in a specific area of your business, consider hiring an EA with relevant experience.

For example, when I first started Michael Hyatt & Company, Suzie Barbour was one of the EAs paired with me by Belay. I was looking for help with email, calendar, and travel arrangements, and she was great at all that. But she also had a background in human resources, event planning, and operations. Plus, she had managed large teams of executive assistants. When I realized that she could contribute in these areas as well, I began to give her more responsibility. Eventually, I hired her full time and leaned heavily on her HR experience when making our first hires. While still serving as my executive assistant, she hired and trained other EAs, lead our customer service operation, and did our event planning.

If I had tried, during the startup phase, to hire individually for all those competencies, our overhead would have been crushing. Eventually, we hired a full-time team member for HR and moved Suzie into a full-time role in operations. Leaning on a qualified EA helped us scale in a sustainable way.

Do you need some help with financial management? Look for an EA who has supported financial professionals and you'll likely find it. There are many EAs who are experienced in serving real estate professionals, sales professionals, nonprofit leaders, or legal professionals. The possibilities are endless. Whether you need event planning, facilities management, hiring help, or assistance keeping up with customer service emails, the right EA could be a great solution.

◄ *EA Power Tip No. 4* ►
Delegate the Creation
JIM KELLY
Executive Assistant to Michael Hyatt, CEO

A lot of leaders hesitate to hire an assistant—or delegate something to their assistant—because they think they first need to set up the templates or systems themselves. But you can actually have your assistant do that for you!

A world-class EA can create a first draft of an email or a template for you to edit. They can meet with you in person or over the phone to discover your expectations, then draft a workflow or system based on your instructions.

Don't let the lack of a process get in the way of your delegation. A good assistant can set up the templates and processes for you.

It's a Wonderful Role

I started the prior chapter with a reference to black-and-white movies, which can give us outdated images of the scope of an EA's contribution. But here's a movie reference still relevant, especially to the topic of the EAs and the essential role they can play in our lives.

You've probably seen Frank Capra's holiday classic, *It's a Wonderful Life*. When the main character, George Bailey, decides the world would be better off without him, an angel named Clarence shows him how much his life really matters. How? Clarence subtracts Bailey from his own life, then leads him through his hometown of Bedford Falls, New York.

Bailey's world looks very different without him. People aren't as successful as they otherwise would have been. They're poorer, bitterer, and live under the control of Mr. Potter, a rent-seeking slumlord who despises George's company for its promotion of middle-class independence through home ownership. By seeing what things would look like without his small efforts, George Bailey finally understands the vital role that he has played. Not surprisingly, he becomes eager to get back to the real Bedford Falls and keep on living his "wonderful life."

I love that story, even though it can seem a bit sappy and sentimental. George Bailey's life was filled with the same kinds of struggles and sacrifices we all make. Burdened by the demands of his business, he never found the time to fulfill his dream of traveling the world. In big ways and small ways, we are all George Bailey at one point or another. We all make a key difference in the lives of others—and they do in our lives as well.

It's a valuable exercise to look at where you are and imagine how things might have gone differently if one player or another were never there to begin with. Think about your own life and career. Was there a George Bailey—a teacher, parent, mentor, friend—who provided something that was missing from your life, enabling you to be more successful and fulfilled? I'll bet there was.

As you mentally strip the George Baileys away from your life, you'll likely get further and further away from what you have achieved so far. In that spirit, I can say that I never would have accomplished what I have without the EAs who helped me along the way. They've played pivotal roles in my success.

I would not have succeeded as CEO of Thomas Nelson without my EA, nor would I have founded Platform University, started several podcasts, launched the Full Focus Planner and programs like The Focused Leader and BusinessAccelerator. In short, there would be no Michael Hyatt and Company today if not for the help and support of dozens of others, including some world-class EAs.

Having the right people in your life is critical for success, and that includes *your* executive assistant. Getting the help you need is a game changer. So if you're still wondering whether you can "afford" a "secretary," it's time to change your mind-set. You can't afford *not* to partner with a passionate professional who thrives on doing the work that drains and distracts you, enabling you to make a greater contribution than you ever dreamed possible.

You need a world-class executive assistant, and in the next chapter I'll show you how to find one.

PART 2

The Relationship

CHAPTER 4

Hiring the Right Executive Assistant

A good rule of thumb when hiring an executive assistant is that if you think you might need one, you actually needed one six months ago. When you end your work day knowing that you haven't accomplished the things that matter most, when you feel overwhelmed for long stretches, when you have more items on your task list every morning that you can possibly accomplish, it's past time to hire an EA.

This chapter is about the right way to start, but the first and most important step is to start somewhere.

Decide you need help, and then go out and get the help that you need without delay. Every day you wait puts you further behind. If you want to end the overwhelm, you need to take action. The good news? Your world-class assistant may be easier to find than you think.

We'll begin with the two most common questions leaders face in hiring an EA: How much time? and How much money? Then we'll give you tips on where to find the right person and reveal the four key qualities that make an assistant truly world class. If you already have an EA, you'll want to read at least that part of the chapter. It'll be an invaluable tool for evaluating your current EA relationship.

◄ *Are You an EA?* ►

Many of the EAs in our company read the books their leaders are reading. Why? They want to think like their leader thinks so they can better anticipate needs. If you're an EA reading this, good for you! You'll especially want to pay special attention to the four key qualities named in this chapter. Make sure they describe you, and keep them sharp as you continue on your career path. Also, please know that you are one of the George Baileys, making our lives wonderful. We couldn't do it without you! Thanks for your contribution.

The Time/Money Equation

Head count is always an issue in business. From leaders of major corporations to visionary solo-preneurs, every leader feels a bit of hesitation about adding staff—and the costs that come with it. This is especially true for administrative positions, which contribute less directly to the bottom line. It's far easier to justify adding a sales position or technician, for example, because it's easier to see how that will pay off in increased revenue or productivity. Even given the benefits we've seen in Chapters 2 and 3, you may still think you can't afford an EA.

To you, I would respectfully say two things. First, "Yes, you can!" And second, "Start small." Let's talk about the second statement first.

Start Small, Scale Up

Let's say that you're a solopreneur with a decent cash flow and cash reserve, but not an abundance of either. You want to hire someone to free you up for greater achievement, but even a half-time assistant would be a stretch. That's okay! You can get started at whatever level fits right now.

As I've grown my business, I've always been wary of letting investment outpace return. Especially when

I was a solo operator, I needed to make every penny count. That's one reason I was delighted to find Belay, a virtual EA service that allowed me to begin with just a few hours. Some leaders are surprised when I tell them they can contract EA services for as few as ten hours a week, but that's exactly what I did. I saw the benefit right away and increased the hours almost immediately. In the meantime, I was able to get started with a very low level of risk.

If hiring an EA for ten hours a week will move you to action, then start there. Give your quarter-time EA some of the work you've identified as a productivity sinkhole, then evaluate the results. I'm confident you'll not only feel energized but also be much more productive in just a week or two.

Don't stop there. One of the great things about a contracted EA service is that it can scale with you. As your needs grow, you can increase your EA's hours or add a second person. Contract services can even track up and down with your seasonal workload.

Let's say fall and spring are relatively busy seasons for you, but winter and summer slow down a bit. You can start with ten hours of EA services now, ratchet that up to fifteen or twenty hours when you need additional help, and drop back down to ten during the slower times. Is that allowed? Absolutely. A good EA service will work with you to accommodate seasonal needs. Flexibility is one hallmark of a great EA provider. That's one reason it's better to avoid discount EA agencies, which may lack professionalism and versatility. With contract services, as with most other things, you get what you pay for.

If you're like me, you'll notice that you're far more productive in the hours redeemed by using an EA—even if they're few at first. By removing the drudgery and disinterest from your task list, you become even more energized for the tasks in your Desire Zone. Right now, you may be thinking primarily about how to scale down the EA help if you don't need it. But I'll bet within the first month, you'll be looking for ways to scale it up. The returns are that obvious.

Make the Case

Let's move to the question of funding your EA position. If you're in a position that doesn't have EA help, start by helping your employer see the value to them. Your boss won't hire an EA to make your life better. But they'll approve it if they're convinced it will pay off in increased revenue, decreased costs, or both.

One way to do that is to run the delegation math. Melba Duncan, an EA recruiter, points this out in the May 2011 edition of *Harvard Business Review.* Let's say you make $150,000 a year and you could hire an assistant for $50,000. If that assistant can make you a third more productive, they will have paid for themselves. Do the equation using your salary and the likely cost of an assistant. How much is it costing the company for you to schedule your own appointments, type up your own meeting notes, and book your own travel? How much more productive could you be with an EA supporting you for ten hours a week? For twenty?

In reality, an entrepreneur or executive who frees up a third of their workweek will increase their effectiveness by far more than 33 percent. Factor in the increased energy, focus, and margin, and the gains will be much higher. Failing to recognize that is a huge handicap for many businesses, as Duncan points out:

> In their zeal to cut administrative expenses, many companies have gone too far, leaving countless highly paid middle and upper managers to arrange their own travel, file expense reports, and schedule meetings. . . . Generally speaking, work should be delegated to the lowest-cost employee who can do it well. Although companies have embraced this logic by outsourcing work to vendors or to operations abroad, back at

headquarters they ignore it, forcing top talent to misuse their time.

Companies who hire EAs see improved productivity in administrative work *and* greater contributions from leaders who can tap previously unavailable time and energy.

Even in light of the overwhelming justification for hiring executive help, your company, your boss—or maybe even you—may continue to balk at the cost. Here's the thing: there is no reward without risk. At some point, you simply have to take the leap and get the help you need. If your experience is anything like mine, you'll never regret it.

‹ *EA Power Tip No. 5* ›

One EA Can Support Multiple Leaders

ELIZABETH WHITE

*Executive Assistant to Courtney Baker,
Chief Marketing Officer and John Meese,
Brand Director of Platform University*

A lot of leaders hesitate to hire an assistant because they're not sure if they need someone full-time. The great news is that a single assistant can actually support multiple leaders!

Right now, I divide my time evenly between

John and Courtney. We follow a fluid format where, instead of having set hours for each leader, I manage my own schedule to best fit each of their needs. Some days I'll spend more time on Courtney's projects, and other days John's work takes center stage.

You could follow a more structured model for sharing an EA's time, allocating certain hours of the day or days of the week to each leader. Whichever approach you take, having one assistant support two leaders is a great way to get the help you need even before you're ready to hire someone full-time.

How to Find the Right EA

You're ready to hire an EA. Congratulations! But where will you find that world-class assistant? It'll be easier than you might think. People with the skills and character to be rock-star EAs may be right in front of you. If you have an HR department, you'll need to work within their established systems for hiring. Even so, you can work with them to ensure the successful candidate displays the characteristics you're looking for.

If you, like most entrepreneurs and leaders of small-but-growing businesses, don't have HR support, no worries. These tips will help you get started.

Start with a Job Description

I've linked to a sample job description in the Resources section of this book. It's the one we used in a recent search that resulted in hiring our CFO, Jarrod Souza. You can use it as a template to design a position description for your EA, or any other position for that matter. It's okay if you don't have all the answers right now. In fact, it's wise to limit yourself to a page or so of notes so the description isn't too complex. You're looking for clarity on the top few things your EA must be able to do and the competencies and characteristics that go with them.

Start by listing the top five tasks you want to delegate. These will probably come straight from your Drudgery Zone. Take note of the skills and abilities that would describe someone who excels at those tasks. If you want to do a deep dive on that, I recommend the Kolbe A Assessment and Kolbe RightFit, which I'll say more about later in the chapter.

Once you've determined what your EA will do for you, it's time to find the right person for the job. But before you begin searching, there are two more things to consider.

Consider Using an EA Service

The first thing to consider is whether you will make use of a contracting service or hire an employee.

Contracting with an EA service is a great option for many people. Most services are simple to engage and highly customizable. It takes much of the effort out of hiring an EA, especially a part-timer. If you use an EA service, especially one that focuses on remote support, you don't have to worry about several things, such as providing office space and equipment, creating personnel policies, screening candidates, rate setting, and payroll management. The service provider handles all that.

But there are trade-offs. The relationship you have with a contractor will be different than the one that you have with employees. Contractors tend to be temporary and may have a lower investment in your success than employees do. That doesn't mean one relationship is better than the other. They just function in different ways to meet different needs.

Even if you intend to hire a full-time employee at some point, it may be wise to begin with a contractor so you can evaluate both the person and the kind of working relationship you want to establish with your assistant. In my company, we continue to use contrated EAs on an as-needed basis. On more than one occasion, we have gone on to hire them as full-time employees.

The real advantage to using an EA service is that you get nearly instant access to a solid assistant who's been pre-screened and trained. And if the relationship doesn't work out, no worries. The services I know are happy to change the personnel they provide based on client satisfaction.

Consider Local vs. Remote Help

A second thing to consider is whether you'll use a local or a remote EA. I've done both, and each brings pluses and minuses. At Michael Hyatt & Company, we started with an all-virtual team. As we've grown, we've developed a hybrid model. All of our EAs live in the area, but attendance at our shared workspace is discretionary. That means our EAs (and all employees, for that matter) sometimes work remotely from their homes and sometimes join us in the office, depending on the needs of their boss and the tasks for the day. We think that offers the best of both worlds, but both local and remote options have advantages.

A locally based EA can be available for in-person meetings, which is often an advantage. They can also run errands, more easily perform clerical tasks such as copying and mailing, collaborate directly with team members, wrangle office equipment, and pick up on cues or details that might be missed via phone or video conference. The great disadvantage is the need to provide office space, which is especially difficult in a startup.

Remote work offers real advantages also. Most tasks that your EA will handle can be done from home, such as communication, document management, participation in video meetings, research, vendor management, and online shopping. Remote employees usually appreciate the freedom to flex their schedule a bit and avoid commuting. They may actually be more productive in some ways because of the decreased time spent on office interactions.

However, the downside is a sense of isolation and the lack of face-to-face contact, which can be important for the working relationship. By instituting a clear communication rhythm and providing some opportunities for team interaction, even by video, those problems can be overcome.

Find Your EA

If you've decided to use a contract EA service and settled the question of local versus remote support, you're ready to make the call and engage an assistant right away. But if you're looking for a regular employee, full-or part-time, remote or local, your next task is recruiting.

Sometimes finding the right candidate is as simple as working your networks. There are a number of ways to do this. One is to query your tribe on social media. You might be surprised at the number of friends who know someone with the right aptitude and experience for this work. Your world-class assistant could be just one degree of separation away.

Crowdsourcing also ensures that you get pre-qualified candidates. Presumably, the members of your tribe know something about your product, your character, and your values. They're likely to recommend only people who they think would be a good fit.

Some entrepreneurs and executives worry that doing this will attract more fans than serious applicants, but that fear is usually misplaced. It's a good thing if people who are applying for jobs know your brand and use your products. That's an advantage that will make training easier. It's a huge help.

You can put out the same call for referrals to your team. Let them do some recruiting for you. They know your product and workstyle even better, and they'll recommend only people they'd be happy to see on the team.

If neither your tribe nor your team turn up enough qualified prospects, you can always list the job publicly. If you have an HR department, they'll likely handle that. If you do not have HR support, check on the basic legal requirements for hiring in your jurisdiction to ensure your posting and hiring practice is compliant with the law.

4 Key Qualities

Whether you hire your own EA or use a contractor, and regardless of the specific responsibilities you plan to delegate, you're looking for a person who can do more than just handle the assignment. Skill is important, but it's just the starting point for a world-class assistant. Your ideal candidate must possess four key qualities if they're to become a solid partner in your work. They are skills, aptitude, attitude, and character. You can test for the first two, and there are some other ways to get rough measures of the rest.

Skills

What skills will your EA need? That'll depend on the specific tasks you want to delegate to them. You may need an EA who is ridiculously good at scheduling. Or you may need someone who excels at maintaining processes but won't be needed to screen calls. And what about areas of competency that fall outside what you might normally consider an EA's purview, things like HR support, light bookkeeping, or project management? One size does not fit all.

In other words, you may be looking at a very different person from the EA who serves one of your colleagues, even though they'll carry the same job title. That's why getting crystal clear on the job description is so important. The tasks you ask them to do will dictate the skills required. But how do you verify that the candidate can do the job?

Beyond reviewing their resume and checking references, you can test for the skills you want. We routinely ask candidates who have passed our first round of interviews to take a skills test. When this goes beyond the time that might be required for a normal interview, we actually compensate them. If your EA must be able to tame a chaotic calendar, you can ask them to sort out the next month of your actual calendar, making choices according to your priorities. If they must be able to engage on social media, ask them to compose a dozen tweets or Instagram posts. Any skill can be tested. If no standard test exists, create your own based on real-life tasks your EA will be expected to perform.

Aptitude

A brief test assignment should give you an indication of whether or not your candidate has the chops for a task. But there's more to success than learned skill. There is also aptitude. Aptitude is that seemingly natural inclination or innate ability to perform certain work or to learn it quickly. It's what we sometimes call having a knack for a particular task or type of work.

It is important to determine, as best you can, the aptitude of your EA for the work you have in mind. The problem with measuring aptitude is that it's often done with personality assessments, and many commonly used assessments have proven to have a built-in bias based on race, age, or gender. That's makes them unsuitable to use in employment settings, especially for hiring.

At Michael Hyatt & Company, the assessment we've come to rely on most in hiring is the Kolbe A Index. While other assessments examine intelligence or personality, the Kolbe A assesses the way our minds work when approaching a task. In other words, it's not about how we think or feel, but how we *go about our work.* So far, it has never been proven to be biased concerning race, age, or gender. The Kolbe A gives us a good idea whether or not a person has the aptitude for, say research (which requires an aptitude for fact finding), or process creation (high on follow through), or clerical work (which involves using their hands a lot).

Attitude

Attitude is harder to screen for than skills or aptitude, but it's vital. You may want an EA who challenges you at times. For instance, let's say you have your EA handle your schedule. It could be valuable for that EA to push back; for instance, when you attempt to add something else to the schedule, you may want someone who will tell you if they believe you are cannibalizing your important priorities or margin.

If you'd like an EA to advocate on your behalf, challenge the status quo, or help you manage others, it's wise to get someone who has some leadership traits. But what kind of traits and how do you screen for it?

You want people who embrace the model of servant leadership. The concept was named by a man named Robert Greenleaf. He worked for AT&T for decades. Greenleaf observed that the leadership of many companies in the middle of the twentieth century were too interested in the accumulation of status and power and not focused enough on serving others. He resolved to do something about that.

Greenleaf took early retirement from AT&T and began writing, speaking, and consulting on how the more top-down models of leadership were dead wrong, for their employees and for their customers. His challenge continues to resonate with many companies to this day. The Robert K. Greenleaf Center for Servant Leadership says that a servant-leader "focuses primarily on the growth and well-being of people and the communities to which they belong."

Practically, what servant-leadership means in an EA is that you want someone who is confident and capable and humble. This is the kind of EA for whom the following two statements are true:

"I have employed [my EA] for a number of years. There was an important meeting in my company that had to happen, but I took ill at the last minute. It was not a good idea to cancel, so I asked [them] to run it, and it was a success."

"People told me there was one presenter at that meeting who had a persistent cough. [They] went and grabbed a glass of water for that presenter, the cough settled down, and the meeting continued without a hitch."

That's a servant leader and then some: One who is capable of running a meeting in your absence or confident enough to push back about your overbooked schedule, but who remains humble enough to pick up your dry cleaning or get a glass of water for someone who needs it. How do you screen for that? It's not as easy as screening for skills or aptitudes, but it is possible.

First, ask the right questions in the interview. These can range from open-ended questions such as,

"What is leadership?" to more specific ones about what experiences made them want to be an EA. In my company, we use a standard set of questions for every EA interview, which are designed to screen for attitude. There's a link to this in the Resources section.

Second, have several other people interview the prospective EA. This is straightforward enough if you're part of a larger company, but it is also possible if you're a solopreneur. I've had my wife Gail talk with prospective EAs, for instance.

Third, call the people listed as references and ask about their impressions of the candidate, rather than performance. Describe the attitude you're looking for, and ask if you have just described the candidate. If they jump in with concrete examples, you may have a winner.

Character

Last but definitely not least is character. Every EA occupies a position of extreme trust. They will often have access to privileged information, trade secrets, financial data, addresses, IDs, passwords, and credit cards. While it is routine to have them sign a nondisclosure agreement as part of the onboarding process (more on that in the next chapter), the threat of legal sanctions may not deter a bad actor. I wish I didn't have to say this, but part of the screening process should be a criminal background check.

Beyond that, be alert when checking references for any hint that the candidate is not worthy of a very high level of trust. And when you and others are interviewing, ask questions that look beyond the resume and see where character shows up. For example, you might say, "When is it okay to break the rules? Give an example of when it is appropriate to do this and explain why." The candidate's answer to this question will shed light on their decision making, emotional intelligence, and character. Successful responses might include examples of breaking the rules when someone was in physical danger or had violated ethics or confidentiality standards.

Finally, I always coach leaders to "hire slow." By now you probably feel some urgency to find an assistant and get them working. But don't be too hasty. Hiring the wrong person is worse than hiring no one. Conduct a thorough search and screening process, and you're very likely to be happy with the result.

You can do this! The right person is out there, and may be closer than you think. To ensure the success of your company, reach your personal goals, and protect your own well-being, you need the help of a world-class assistant. And in the next chapter, I'll show you how to ensure their success with a seamless onboarding process. Already have an EA? This will be a great way to bring them up to speed on what you need in this new phase of working together.

CHAPTER 5

Working Together

Equipping to Win

One reason EA relationships suffer and sometimes fail is that drowning leaders simply pull their assistant into the deep end with them. No onboarding. No training. Just a task dump and a pat on the back. I understand that temptation. And a good EA probably does too. They know you're busy—that's why they signed on to help.

A competent assistant will manage under those circumstances, but the results won't be nearly as good as they could be if you'd taken some time to prepare them to win. That goes for new hires, of course, but also for an EA you already have. If you've never taken the time to properly equip them, now's the time to do it.

You'll get the best results if you and your EA both set clear expectations, and if you given them the information they need to succeed. This is also a great way to quickly improve an existing EA relationship. And since EAs can't read minds, the onboarding begins with a massive information download.

Information Sharing

Most leaders share their contacts and schedule with an EA, though that's just a starting point. Your EA will need access to a host of details from the get-go, and it can be a lot to take in. Too much, really. It's not wise to just spew information as it comes to mind, hoping your EA can keep up. Instead, I suggest creating a document that collects all the information your EA will need about you. Most of that information is confidential, but if you've screened properly, you'll have an assistant you can trust—plus a signed nondisclosure agreement. If you're using an EA service, they should already have covered these issues on your behalf.

How much you share is your call, but there is almost no such thing as too much information on this document. The more information you give your

EA, the better they'll be able to assist you. Some of the things to include are your full name; birthday; photos of your driver's license, passport, or other forms of identification; the credit card number they'll use to make your business purchases, and the one for personal purchases; names and birthdays of family members; your anniversary; where the children go to school; doctor's office or other medical contacts; favorite lunch and dinner spots; what you like to order at those restaurants; your standard coffee order; your gym and usual workout days; preferred airline, frequent flier number, and seating preferences; customer loyalty numbers for hotels and car rental companies. I told you it was a lot.

Thankfully, we've developed a tool to help you capture all this data in a handy format. At Michael Hyatt & Company, our EAs manage a spreadsheet containing all the relevant information for their bosses. There's a link to this document in the Resources section. You can download and customize it as needed. This will save you both a lot of time.

This spreadsheet houses a ton of sensitive information, so you'll want to have your EA store it in a secure folder and password protect it. I recommend meeting with your EA when you first begin your relationship and have them interview you to get all of this information. This will save you time, and it will enable them to begin managing the information, scheduling, and making decisions on your behalf.

◄ EA Power Tip No. 6 ►

Communicate Expectations and Preferences

SUSAN CALDWELL
Personal Assistant to Gail Hyatt

If you're hesitating to delegate something, it's often because you're worried it won't be done the way you want. That's why it's so important to communicate your expectations and your preferences.

Take a few minutes to list your expectations and preferences before your EA starts a project. Tell them when you need it complete. Tell them what options they should definitely consider—and which ones they shouldn't. Tell them how much detail you want in the end. Gail, for example, wants all the information about the project, while other leaders want just the big picture. And tell your EA how much authority they have to make decisions.

It's true that your assistant isn't a mind reader. But if you give them enough clarity about what you prefer, they'll be able to execute as though they were!

The Executive Information Spreadsheet

The spreadsheet has several tabs, organized by various life domains. This gives the context for various contacts, which enables an EA to execute faster and more effectively.

Tab 1: Personal

The first tab is all about you, starting with your full name, date of birth, social security number, driver's license number, email addresses, contact information, and miscellaneous preferences such as what size clothes you wear, your favorite color, what stores you frequent, your hobbies or interests, and any allergies or dietary restrictions. Things like clothing size and favorite color may seem trivial or unimportant, but if you're traveling and lose your suitcase and then need to have clothes ordered to make it to a meeting, then that information is already available, and your EA can go to work solving your problem instead of having to ask you for all of this information during a stressful situation.

Tab 2: Family

The second tab includes info about your spouse

and kids: names, contact information, and the rest, including your spouse's preferences. This will help with choosing gifts on your behalf: particular flower arrangements or florists, favorite coffee order, what restaurants they enjoy. You also want to give any information that helps you run your household: numbers for babysitters, schools, vet, pet groomers, and so on. And don't stop there. Include info on your adult children if you have any, parents, in-laws, and so on. List any information your EA would need to accomplish a task for you without coming to you with repeated questions.

Tab 3: Travel

Travel can be stressful, but with the right information your EA can smooth some of the bumps. Share your Global Entry number, preferred airline, and so on. Preferences are really important here. Share your preferred class, seats (for instance, bulkhead, exit row, aisle, window), transportation (rental, Uber, car service), and hotels (brand, room selection, upper or lower floor). Break these out by cities you regularly visit. Don't forget your travel account information: websites, login information, email, passwords, or account numbers. Sharing PIN numbers is also helpful, especially customer loyalty accounts. It's a good idea to include credit card authorizations here as well. This information will help your EA reliably book any travel you need.

Tab 4: Money

The next tab over contains all the financial information your EA would need to make decisions and purchases on your behalf: personal banking info and credit card numbers, company accounts and credit cards, along with any reporting software your assistant might need to log expenses.

Tab 5: Social Media

The next tab is for any social media information you want to share. Having your EA manage your accounts is a great way to decrease your distraction, especially if you are the public face of your brand, or if you need help maintaining a posting schedule and making replies to your clients or fan base. You stay connected without giving up your valuable time.

Tab 6: Restaurants

The next tab over covers your preferences for eating out. Instead of having to ask for this information every time, your EA will have a handy list of your favorite restaurants, usual orders, standard coffee order, and, just as important, the places you'd like to avoid. It's also a good idea to reiterate dietary restrictions or allergies here as well.

Tab 7: Medical

The next tab is for medical appointments, along with any other health-related information worth sharing. Share your medical, dental, and vision insurance. Share contact info for your primary care physician, dentist, chiropractor, and any other health professional you see. Add any health concerns you might have, so your EA can be conversant when they set up appointments. And throw in your blood type; you never know when that might come in handy.

Tab 8: Vendors

The next tab is for any vendors that you deal with regularly: your accountant, your lawyer, your gym, your dry cleaner, your stylist or barber, home repair services, and so on. Include any miscellaneous contact information your EA might need to set up appointments. After you've shared all this information, you don't have to worry whether they know who to call when you need something done.

Tab 9: Passwords

The final tab in the spreadsheet is for other passwords and account information not already captured for, say, websites you regularly use, subscriptions, and the like. You can also do this with a little more control, security, and centralization through an app like 1Password, which enables the sharing of specific passwords, and allows you to revoke access at any time. It also simplifies password updates and two-factor authentication.

◄ *EA Mistake No. 3* ►

Hoarding Information

Some of us don't share our lives enough with our EAs. We could delegate much more if we were more transparent about both our work and home life. A good EA will see where they can help with things we didn't realize could be delegated. But that only happens if we give them access. How many unnecessary tasks and low-payoff activities could you offload if you would simply give your EA the permission to take them?

Granting Access

In addition to helping your EA become an expert on you by providing as much information as possible up front, you want to ensure that your EA has ongoing access to you. An EA cannot perform well in isolation. Here are some things you can do at the outset to establish your relationship on the right footing.

Be Available

We'll go in-depth on EA communication strategies in the next chapter, but at the start it's critically important to be responsive to questions. Provide more context than you think is needed. Over communicate. Your EA needs more time from you in the beginning in order to save you time in the long-run.

Release Control

We've talked a lot about how EAs can manage your calendar and your email, and how they can take over expense reporting and be responsible for some personal administrative tasks. Don't resist handing these things over to your EA. Onboarding is the time to delegate all of these responsibilities. Certainly, more items will surface as you move along. But letting go of your calendar, for example, displays great trust and establishes a solid working relationship. For some of us, it's a real struggle to let go of these tasks. But your world-class assistant is more than capable of handling them, probably better than you're now doing.

Communicate your vision and expectations, then hand these tasks over.

Clarify Your Style

Just as you were eager to learn your EA's skills, aptitude, attitude, and character, they're interested in knowing these things about you. One quick tool for clarifying your leadership style for others—and for yourself—is the LeaderScore Assessment. This is a tool I developed for my coaching clients that will score your leadership against nine metrics of success. This helps you dial in on your leadership skills and aptitudes, and you can share this information with your EA. Don't be intimidated by that. First of all, your EA will spot your strengths and weaknesses in time anyway. And the more they know about you, the more tasks they can take over to mitigate your weaknesses and support your strengths. There's a link for this tool in the Resources section.

Broaden Their Training

I've seen many leaders hire an EA because they're desperate for help, then rush through the onboarding process—or skip it entirely. That doesn't serve the leader well in the long run, and it's exhausting for the EA. Your assistant needs to know both you and your team, your leadership style, and the company culture. When your EA understands company processes, is introduced to key leaders, peers, and clients, and has a sense of "how we do things here," they'll be much more effective. Though your EA is hired to help you, they need exposure to others as well.

The First Ninety Days

What you do in the first ninety days with your EA will set the tone of the relationship for the balance of your time together and determine whether you can really achieve something great as a team. Invest time and energy in this relationship on the front end, and it will pay dividends for years to come.

There's always a learning curve, of course. Discovering someone's preferences, strengths, weaknesses, and workstyle takes time—for both of you. Getting your EA up to speed requires a little patience. This can be hard for some leaders, especially those who are most overwhelmed and feel the urgency to get help *now.*

Take your time. Remember, this relationship is not just about you; it's about your EA too. When you hoard tasks and information, you communicate a lack of trust. So let go. When you are unavailable for questions, you signal that it's sink-or-swim. So check in. When you take back a task you've delegated because it's not done as quickly or as well as you'd hoped, you demoralize your EA. So communicate and coach.

Stick with this process. You're on the verge of finding the freedom you have longed for to invest in your high-leverage tasks and really see your business grow. And in the next chapter, I'll show you the advanced techniques that will help you fully leverage the power of your world-class assistant.

◄ *EA Mistake No. 4* ►

Hoarding Tasks

Some of us actually like managing our inboxes and schedules; others are just control freaks. Either way, it sucks up tons of time that could be used for high-leverage activities. The main culprits here are email and calendar management. Leaders who refuse to delegate these two functions are killing their own productivity.

CHAPTER 6

Working Together

Communication and Delegation

You probably got where you are today because of your commitment, grit, and get-it-done attitude. That's enough gas to get most of us down the road toward our goals. But it's never enough to go all the way. There will always be more things to do, but there will only be one you. That's why you need to develop the skill of delegation, and the prerequisite for that is clear communication. As we continue looking at how leverage the power of an executive assistant, we'll address both.

Communication Rhythms

If you are married, the two most important people to communicate with on a day-to-day basis are your spouse and your EA. If you are not married, then your EA is the most important person, hands down.

Use your words. Use lots of them. And never ghost your EA. There's no such thing as over-communication, especially at the beginning of the working relationship. It's easy to say, but it's also easily overlooked for the sake of time and urgency. Listen: If your spouse can't read your mind after however many years of marriage, what makes you think your EA can?

There may be a suite of tools that you already prefer to use for email, company chat, project management, video conferencing, file sharing, and calendar management. If so, equip your EA with these tools right away. If not, experiment with tools together to see what works. The best tools should be easy to use and facilitate frictionless communication between you and your EA. I recommend several tools, which we use at Michael Hyatt & Company, listed in the Resources section.

Beyond intentions and tools, it helps to have a plan for regular communication. Think of them as rituals or standing appointments that become part of your Ideal Week. I recommend both a weekly one-on-one and daily check-ins. Along with that, you'll also want a plan for as-needed and emergency communication.

◄ *EA Mistake No. 5* ►

Under Communicating

Communication is key to working with an EA, yet I constantly see EA relationships that suffer because leaders fail to provide necessary details about their work and even their private lives. If an EA is a partner in achieving our goals, they will only be as effective as they are dialed into what's happening. Keeping them in the dark only hurts our ability to succeed.

Weekly One-on-One

I suggest that you set up a standing, weekly one-on-one meeting with your EA, whether remote or in-person—and do not miss this. This meeting is only partly on day-to-day business. The other part, which you should not neglect, is managing bigger picture EA issues: progress on goals and projects, scheduling issues, the size of the overall workload (for both of you), and how that is being managed.

This is the time when the two of you poke your heads above the clouds and look at the next several weeks—take a measure of the landscape. You will manage this meeting at the start, but, over time, it may be useful to let your EA set the agenda. That's what I do. I've included our regular one-on-one agenda in the back of the book.

Jim and I start with "positive focus." We look at some of our accomplishments and wins from the last week, in both our professional and personal lives. That puts any problems in perspective and sets the tone for a positive, constructive meeting.

Next, we review the calendar together. Usually both of us have the calendar open so we can confer on what we see. We look for red flags: where meetings are too tightly scheduled, or when I need materials to review in advance of an event, and so on. Since Jim manages my calendar (see Chapter 3), he often books meetings I'm not aware of. This is his chance to bring me up to speed. This is also a good time to review upcoming priorities—my Weekly Big 3 tasks necessary to make progress on my goals and key projects—and decide if anything needs to move to accommodate them.

After that, we troubleshoot issues that require more conversation than could easily happen in a Slack thread. Jim might have just a couple of questions, but sometimes it's as many as ten. He cuts and pastes these into the calendar invitation for the meeting. This is a great opportunity to discuss outstanding email requests that we need to confer about before responding. The regular one-on-one provides a predictable time for getting necessary answers. We close with a recap of the action items Jim has asked me to handle or that I've delegated to him.

Usually this meeting is roughly thirty minutes long. The important thing to note is that you can make this meeting whatever you need it to be. One of the executives on our team follows the Full Focus Planner's "Weekly Preview" with his EA as the agenda for their one-on-one. Another follows a simple, four-part framework: updates, questions, decisions, and action items.

Some questions you or your EA might use to get you started: Do you have any concerns about any of these events? Do we need to change or reschedule anything? Is there anything we need to cancel? Listen if your EA pushes back on your plans. They usually have a better grasp of your calendar and how much time things will take than you do.

Daily Check-ins

Another helpful way to connect are daily check-ins in the morning or afternoon—or both. You can tackle smaller or more pressing questions than you might cover in your weekly one-on-one.

◄ *EA Power Tip No. 7* ►

Have a Weekly One-on-One

BECCA TURNER

Executive Assistant to Chad Cannon
Chief Sales Officer

If you're a leader and sometimes feel out of sync with your assistant, you're not alone. It can be tough to find an efficient way to stay on the same page. At Michael Hyatt & Company, we use weekly one-on-ones to make that a breeze. It's a quick touchpoint you can count on every week.

It's helpful to have a standing agenda so you know what to expect—and so none of the important details are left out. Chad and I use a four-part agenda: updates, questions, decisions, action items. There may be others that are relevant for you. Having a regular check-in with a reliable agenda will ensure that you and your assistant are perfectly in sync.

When I ask our executives or those we coach how long their daily check-ins are, the time ranges from ten to twenty minutes, sometimes as long as thirty. If that seems like a big commitment every day, consider how much time it actually saves. A quick review of the schedule, outstanding requests and decisions, email and voicemail requests, and doing this as part of your workday startup ritual means you're free to jump right in on your top priorities of the day. Doing that as part of your workday shutdown means you can close the mental loops and fully unplug, leaving you fully present with family or friends after work.

Our COO, Megan Hyatt Miller, will often do a daily check in with her EA, Jamie, from the car on her way to and from the office. Jim and I do it a little differently, using a Slack app called Geekbot. Every morning Geekbot asks us both the following questions:

- How do you feel today?

- What are your Daily Big 3?

- Anything blocking your progress?

The Daily Big 3 are the three most important tasks for each day, which are usually informed by my Weekly Big 3. When our answers are posted in Slack, we can elaborate or ask additional questions as needed. It's a great way for us to touch base without necessarily taking time on a phone call or waiting until our next one-on-one.

We have a slightly different Geekbot question-and-answer on Mondays. We ask, "What are your Weekly Big 3 for this week?" We also discuss these in our weekly one-on-one, but we post them here to get the ball rolling.

◄ *EA Power Tip No. 8* ►

Communication Strategies

ALESHIA CURRY

Assistant to Joel Miller,
Chief Content Officer

Most leaders deal with an avalanche of communications every day. When you're constantly answering questions, communicating with your EA can feel like a drain. But if you're smart about communicating with your assistant, they can actually minimize the rest of that noise for you. Joel and I use three tactics for daily communications that will help you, too. First, share your priorities for the day and week with your assistant. (At Michael Hyatt & Co., we call this your Weekly and Daily Big 3.) That helps your assistant defend time for those priorities.

Second, open a channel of communication where your assistant can reach you for critical answers. If you're not responsive to anyone else, answer your EA.

Third, empower your EA to answer communications for you. Tell them which meeting requests they should always accept—or always decline. Tell them which emails and questions they're authorized to answer. When you empower your EA to answer most of the requests—and create a reliable channel where they can get your input on the rest—you'll be unburied in no time.

As-needed and Emergency Communication

Mike Tyson said, "Everyone's got a plan until they get punched in the mouth." Hello, Tuesday! Since emergencies and other special situations pop up all the time, it's important that you have an understanding with your EA on what constitutes emergency communication and how it should work.

For instance, at Michael Hyatt & Company we encourage our teams to disconnect on nights and weekends. If someone posts an emergency message in Slack after hours, odds are good no one will see it. So if there's an emergency, we use text messages and jump on the phone or Slack if necessary. If you're disconnecting for some deep work, you'll want a plan for that as well. Even if no one else can reach you, you'll want your EA to have a way to get in touch with you.

Since the substance of much of this communication will involve delegation, it's important we address that next step.

Delegation Basics

Delegation is a complicated subject. I could write a whole book on it. (And, who knows, I just might!) There's a lot more to doing it successfully than simply assigning projects. For now, we'll focus on the stages of delegation, the levels of delegation, and the difference between delegation and abdication.

◄ EA Mistake No. 6 ►

Failing to Delegate

If there's a secret sauce to leadership, it's delegation. Nothing will sink a leader faster than the inability to assign priorities and responsibilities. Contrary to what you may have thought, delegation is not an innate ability. It's a skill anyone can learn. But many of us don't. So we fail to delegate properly to the one person working closest to us, our EA. That's a recipe for disaster. One EA was straightforward about the problem: "If you don't ask for something to be done and then explain how you'd like it accomplished, I'm no good to you!"

The Stages of Delegation

It's easy to assume the right way to start is to dump all of your nonessential tasks on your new EA all at once, then be done with it. Do that only if you want to complicate your life. Even the best EAs have learning curves. As they do one task more and more, they get smarter about it and better at it. As they get better at a task, the time to get that task done shortens. This means they have more time to take on additional tasks.

If you just take your big box of tasks and dump those on a new EA's desk, you are not doing either one of you any favors. Even if this EA can eventually shoulder this workload, that's unlikely to be the case right out of the box. And by dumping tasks out indiscriminately, you are making it difficult to focus on one task at a time and master it, which would make room for more work. You are doing something that just might lengthen the learning curve for every single task.

If you want to avoid overwhelming your new EA, or if you already have an EA that you haven't been great about delegating to, try delegating in stages. Have your EA tackle a few tasks, allow some time, add a few more tasks, then pause and evaluate.

I have good news for you: You already made up the blueprint for how to do this in Chapter 1, when you listed all of your tasks and ranked them according to the Freedom Compass Zones. The first candidates for delegation are in Zone 4, the Drudgery Zone. Delegating these tasks will offer the quickest relief because you're neither good at nor enjoy them.

Once your EA has mastered these tasks, move on to Zone 2, Distraction Zone tasks. These will be harder to let go because, even if you lack proficiency, you enjoy them. However, because you lack proficiency, you're not adding much value by holding on to these items. And because you enjoy them, chances are good you're only doing them to avoid harder but more valuable work.

After Zone 4 and Zone 2 tasks, it's time to start off-loading Zone 3, the Disinterest Zone. The goal here is to work on tasks that are primarily in Zone 1, your Desire Zone. That may take more players than just one EA, so it'll take time and scaling to get there. In the meantime, it's important to restate that you'll be tempted to push too much on your EA too quickly, just for the feeling of relief. Don't. It's an illusion, and you'll burn up the person who can finally help you see daylight again.

Instead, as you begin, get serious about priorities and opportunity costs. If you ask your EA to do one thing, something else might have to give. It's possible to start off sensibly but lose sight of this over time. As your business grows—as well as your confidence in your EA—you will naturally add more and more tasks. It's very easy to create an impossible scenario with your EA. Make sure you stay in touch with your EA about their workload and believe them when they say they need more hours or some help. You can't afford to overtax one of the most essential roles in your business.

◀ *EA Mistake No. 7* ▶

Offering No Feedback

It's easy to get caught up in the grind and miss opportunities to give our EAs insight into how they're doing or what they could do to improve. This not only hurts our working relationship but also shoots ourselves in the foot. Who benefits if our EA improves? Who suffers if they don't? Regular feedback is a must.

The Five Levels of Delegation

One major reason delegation goes wrong is that leaders don't understand that there are multiple levels of authority and responsibility involved in delegation, that come with varying expectations. It's critical to be clear on the level of authority you are conferring when you delegate a task. Here are the five levels of delegation, and what they mean in practice.

Level 1: Do exactly what I have asked you to do. Don't deviate from my instructions. I have already researched the options and determined what I want you to do.

Level 2: Research the topic and report back. We will discuss it, and then I will make the decision and tell you what I want you to do.

Level 3: Research the topic, outline the options, and make a recommendation. Give me the pros and cons of each option but tell me what you think we should do. If I agree with your decision, I will authorize you to move forward.

Level 4: Make a decision and then tell me what you did. I trust you to do the research, make the best decision you can, and then keep me in the loop. I don't want to be surprised by someone else.

Level 5: Make whatever decision you think is best. No need to report back. I trust you completely. I know you will follow through. You have my full support.

Part of the regular communication that you do to make the relationship work should include what level of delegation is attached to a task. To understand these levels in action, imagine I've asked my EA to take dictation for an article on productivity. I may want my words captured precisely and then sent to me to take it from there (Level 1); I may want to look the manuscript over and tell my EA what changes to make and where to send it (Level 2); I may want transcription with suggestions on how to say it better or where to send it, or both (Level 3); I may not want to see the manuscript but want to know where it was sent (Level 4); or I may want my EA to transcribe, edit, and send it to a variety of recipients that I do not specify (Level 5).

Getting the level of delegation right is important in both the short and the long term. In the short term, it makes sure you are on the same page. If all I wanted were comments on my draft article, but instead it was edited and sent to fifteen editors without my knowledge, that would be a pretty clear communication failure.

Delegation levels are important in the long term because one mark of a successful leader-EA relationship is that the EA *levels up* on many tasks. The EA goes from "do this exactly as I say" to "do this and report back" or even sometimes just "take care of this, and don't tell me about it." This is a win-win. It shows that the EA has gotten better at tasks and the leader has gotten better at trusting their assistant to assist.

You should also bear in mind and tell your EA that there are some things that *shouldn't* be delegated at a Level 5 grant of authority. This goes to the fundamental role divide between an executive and their assistant. You can outsource all sorts of tasks so you can better fulfill your responsibilities, but the moment you outsource your responsibilities, you've crossed a line.

It might be fine to have my EA edit and place an article for me (Level 5). And it might be a good idea for an EA who has financial chops to scrutinize a company-wide budget for me (Level 3). But as the owner and CEO of the company, it would be something else to tell that EA to approve whichever budget option he thought best for the company, and that I didn't need to know about it. That would be abdication, not delegation.

◀ *EA Mistake No. 8* ▶

Not Providing the Rationale

Mistake No. 4 is related to No. 3. A good EA can fill in the blanks of tasks and projects if they know the rationale behind a task or project. When we don't communicate adequate background and reasoning, we're hampering our EA's ability to help us win. To work independently, an EA must know that why behind the what.

The Risk of Abdication

Not too long ago, I hired a company to completely landscape my backyard. It was a big job, and the contractor projected significant costs and three months to complete it all.

Both estimates were well off the mark. The job ended up taking almost fifteen months. The contractor didn't bill more than he had bid, but I had to hire two other contractors to fix parts of the job he goofed and wouldn't repair. It kills me saying it, but just the salvage job cost an additional seven thousand dollars.

When the job was finally finished, I was angry and wanted to blame the contractor. I thought about writing a negative review on Yelp, complaining to the Better Business Bureau, or even suing him. But then I took a deep breath and asked myself if there was something about my leadership that had led to this drawn-out, expensive outcome? And the question came back: What leadership?

Ultimately, landscaping my yard was still my job. I had only hired somebody to do it on my behalf. The great delays and added expense suggested that I must not have done something important: I didn't provide leadership.

I ought to have stayed on top of the landscaping job. When it approached and then blew past the three-month deadline, I should have had questions for the contractor and prodded him to get the job back on track. Because I didn't do any of that until it was very clear that things had gone badly wrong, I let delegation turn to abdication and paid the price for it.

This disaster had all three classic ingredients of abdication that you'll want to avoid with your EA. Those ingredients are fuzzy goals, poor communication of expectations, and low or no engagement.

Fuzzy Goals: Clarity is vital for leadership, but some of us try to skip this step because it takes focus and time. We get only a vague, fuzzy, general idea in our heads, and proceed from there. Trouble follows.

Poor Communication of Expectations: The second ingredient usually flows from the first. Because we're unclear on what we want, we can't effectively communicate our expectations to others. We don't just task them with filling in some details, we expect them to make up for what is lacking in our vision. Or sometimes we are clear on our vision but do a bad job translating that into expectations for those who are supposed to make it happen. We could quickly correct the miscommunication of clear ideas but for ingredient three.

Low or No Engagement: After we give orders, we physically or mentally vacate. We don't check on progress because we don't want to nag or, frankly, to be bothered. And then we wonder why there are still workers in our backyard six months later.

The answer to the first two problems is a tool I call the Project Vision Caster. There's a link to a sample of this tool in the Resources section in the back of the book. It helps you and your EA get clear on a goal or project, its scope, the rationale for it, and what you expect to have accomplished with the completed project. In other words, it helps you clarify what you want to do, why you want to do it, and what success looks like when it's done. It even includes a place to indicate the delegation level. The answer to the third problem is tracking delegations in your weekly one-on-ones.

Delegation is supposed to free leaders to focus on other priorities. But that only works when we've properly set up the task. Instead, what sometimes happens is that we leave it up to others to make important decisions absent clear instructions and hope it all goes well. Then, when everything goes wrong, we wonder what in the world happened.

Don't make this mistake with your new EA. Too many people try to pile too much on a new EA or aren't clear about how these things are being delegated or they abdicate any responsibility to see that the work gets done, when they could have kept tabs on things by doing something as simple as reviewing assigned tasks in their weekly one-on-one. By neglecting this, they miss out on a lot of the freedom and focus that a good EA makes possible.

CHAPTER 7

Where Next?

A proverbial Japanese industrialist is said to have looked at American corporate culture in the middle of last century and predicted that many firms would have a hard go of it. "Business," the industrialist said, "is now so complex and difficult, the survival of firms so hazardous and fraught with danger, that continued existence depends upon the day-to-day mobilization of every ounce of intelligence."

Management analysts Brian Carney and Isaac Getz expand on that statement in their book *Freedom, Inc.* "Every ounce," they explain, "means every ounce of intelligence," not just in your executives' heads, but "in every brain that comes through the door of your company every day." They warn, "If you are not doing everything you can to take advantage of that brain-power and the knowledge those brains possess about your business, you're not only leaving money on the table, you are putting your company's survival at risk."

A good EA offers more than assistance, they also offer unique intelligence and valuable intellectual capital you can invest in the success of your business. The key to maximizing that investment is becoming an expert at working with your EA. That starts with understanding where you add value—and where you don't. The Freedom Compass will help you with that.

Next, you need to know what kind of value your EA can deliver at the basic and advanced levels. Chapters 2 and 3 can help you with that. This goes for new hires as well as assistants already on the payroll. It's never too late to improve performance—or make a change if necessary. After that, you must properly equip your EA to fulfill the job you've hired them to do. And you must be in regular and effective communication about your calendar, goals, projects, and other delegated tasks.

Beyond that, it's vital to provide feedback and encourage growth in your EA. When we're stuck in the old secretary paradigm, we often undervalue the potential contribution our EAs can make.

In Chapter 1, I mentioned contracting with Belay

for a remote EA. She saved me fifteen hours a week, and it took her only five hours to do the work. Anyone that proficient has something going on. I know a good deal when I see it, so I continued to offload work to her, quickly upping the contract to ten, then fifteen, then twenty hours a week. And then I lost her! Bryan Miles, CEO of Belay, noticed how talented she was and promoted her to COO of his company.

Yet the story has a happy ending for both of us. I took the hint and hired the next EA that Belay sent my way full time. She works for me to this day, but not as an EA. Suzie Barbour demonstrated the kind of talent that warranted promotion. She's now our senior director of operations and helps train all our world-class EAs, whom you've encountered through the book in the EA Power Tips.

An EA is often the answer to the pressing needs of the present. And sometimes they're the answer to as—yet unasked questions about your future as well.

PART 3

The Resources

Key Templates

For downloadable versions of these templates, visit yourworldclassassistant.com/tools.

Your Executive Assistant Job Description

Your Executive Assistant Interview Questions

Job Offer Letter Template

Calendar Proof

Date Night Questions

Event Brief Template

Executive Information Template

Geekbot Questions

Top Ten Email Replies for your Executive Assistant

Your Executive Assistant One-on-One Agenda

Project Vision Caster

Services and Apps

Alfred alfredapp.com

Automates repetitive tasks on your Mac and is especially useful as a search assistant. Alfred is similar to the Spotlight feature built into the Mac OS, but much more versatile.

What We Like: Shortcut keys. Create your own for instant searching.

Asana asana.com

A robust project and task management tool that facilitates collaboration within and between teams. Asana has built-in connectivity to Slack, enabling easy sharing of tasks, information, and assignments.

What We Like: Versatility. Asana works as both a personal task list and a project management tool.

Backblaze backblaze.com

A cloud-based computer backup that runs automatically.

What We Like: No-touch. Just set it, and forget it.

Belay belaysolutions.com

A one-stop solution for finding an experienced, professional virtual assistant to tackle every item in your Drudgery Zone, beginning with as few as ten hours per week.

What We Like: Pre-screening. Belay provides qualified EAs personally selected for your needs.

Boomerang for Gmail boomeranggmail.com

A browser extension that adds non-native features to

Gmail, including scheduled sending, read receipts, and automatic follow-up on unanswered mail.

What We Like: Control. Boomerang lets you determine when others will receive your messages, and lets you know when they've been read.

Calendly calendly.com

Web-based app to help you schedule meetings without the back-and-forth emails.

What We Like: No guesswork. Avoids multiple queries to coordinate meetings.

Evernote evernote.com

A versatile note and document management tool that allows you to easily tag, search, and retrieve data.

What We Like: Photo scanning. Take a picture of your whiteboard diagrams or handwritten notes, and Evernote will digitize the text to make it searchable.

Fantastical flexibits.com/fantastical

Runs on top of Google Calendar and adds many features, including a two-week view, and a clean, pleasing interface.

What We Like: Easy toggling between different calendar sets.

Freedom freedom.to

A tool that uses technology to fight technology. Freedom locks out selected apps or websites when you want intense focus.

What We Like: Syncing. Your settings operate across all your devices.

Geekbot geekbot.com

> A Slack add-on that automates reminders, check-ins, and other communications. Also great for asynchronous standup meetings and in-house surveys or questionnaires.
>
> *What We Like:* Information comes to you. Slackbot will prompt your team to give status updates so you don't have to chase down progress reports.

Google Drive drive.google.com

> A cloud-based document management system that facilitates collaboration. Combined with the G-Suite of products (Sheets, Docs, Slides, Forms), it's a virtual one-stop office.
>
> *What We Like:* Simplicity. It's easy to use, not bloated with complex, seldom-used features.

Google Voice voice.google.com

> A versatile, digital telephone system that automates voicemail, ring schedules, call forwarding, and more.
>
> *What We Like:* Easy on/off. Allows you to easily turn off or forward calls to your public business number, protecting your margin.

Groove groove.co

> An app that integrates sales data, email, and calendar functions to consolidate and simplify your team's email management.
>
> *What We Like:* Time savings. Eliminates manual data entry and keeps all records up to date.

Keyboard Maestro keyboardmaestro.com

A macro processor that automates repetitive tasks on your computer, such as opening certain websites or apps each day.

What We Like: Power. With practice, you can automate highly complex functions with this tool.

Kolbe A Index kolbe.com

A personal assessment that studies how we initiate our work. This index reveals what actions a person is likely to take first when confronted with a new task, such as fact finding versus manual effort.

What We Like: Self-awareness. The Kolbe A helps us and our team members understand one another's work-styles and partner well.

Kolbe RightFit

kolbe.com/genius-network/find-the-rightfit

A statistically proven tool that expedites finding the right person for your role by screening to select applicants who have the necessary instincts.

What We Like: Clarity. Kolbe RightFit takes the guess work out of how a prospective employee will perform within your company's specific job requirements.

LeaderScore Assessment

assessments.michaelhyatt.com/leaderscore

A free online tool to diagnose your strengths and weakness as a leader. Provides nuanced insight into nine key characteristics of leadership.

What We Like: Clarity. Helps both leaders and team

members understand their strengths and weaknesses to improve working relationships.

Loom loom.com

A free, simple tool for making personal videos or screencasts with you in the picture.

What We Like: Personality. Adds warmth and personality by allowing you to address the teammate, client, or customer directly.

Notion notion.so

A powerful database for creating, sorting, and recalling documents. Notion combines the best features of Google Docs, Workflowy, Evernote, and Asana.

What We Like: Versatility. This tool can be used for document creation, task management, and/or team collaboration.

1Password 1password.com

A password vault that enables teams to manage and share logins but revoke access at any time. Also generates super-strong passwords that you never have to memorize.

What We Like: One click. The browser extension fills in login credentials for you.

Slack slack.com

A team communication platform that combines the best aspects of social media and email. Highly versatile, it's great for both all-team, intra-team, and one-on-one messaging.

What We Like: Manageability. Multiple channels

organize messages by topic and threads to keep discussion of individual messages in one place.

SnagIt techsmith.com/screen-capture

A simple solution for creating screenshots and screencasts. Invaluable for creating workflows to be used in delegation.

What We Like: Makes webinar creation a breeze.

Spark spark.com

An email client that operates Gmail and Google Calendar, providing a clean interface and increased functionality.

What We Like: Collaboration. Spark allows team members to discuss the content of an email in a separate window before composing a reply.

TextExpander textexpander.com

Replaces a snippet of your text with anything you choose, from a symbol to a word to a complete sentence, even an entire document.

What We Like: Consistency. Get perfect replication of URLs, product names, contact information, and templates with one or two keystrokes.

Zoom zoom.us

Video conferencing platform with both free and upgraded plans. Also great for webinars and screencasts. Allows participation by guests via the web app.

What We Like: Simplicity and reliability. Zoom is easy to use and never lets you down.